Telepathy

Increase Your Mind Power and Connect to Your Spirit Guide

(Discover the Secrets of Kundalini Awakening and Become a Highly Sensitive Person)

Shante Toledo

Published By **Tyson Maxwell**

Shante Toledo

All Rights Reserved

Telepathy: Increase Your Mind Power and Connect to Your Spirit Guide (Discover the Secrets of Kundalini Awakening and Become a Highly Sensitive Person)

ISBN 978-1-998901-14-2

No part of this guidebook shall be reproduced in any form without permission in writing from the publisher except in the case of brief quotations embodied in critical articles or reviews.

Legal & Disclaimer

The information contained in this ebook is not designed to replace or take the place of any form of medicine or professional medical advice. The information in this ebook has been provided for educational & entertainment purposes only.

The information contained in this book has been compiled from sources deemed reliable, and it is accurate to the best of the Author's knowledge; however, the Author cannot guarantee its accuracy and validity and cannot be held liable for any errors or omissions. Changes are periodically made to this book. You must consult your doctor or get professional medical advice before using any of the suggested remedies, techniques, or information in this book.

Table Of Contents

Chapter 1: A Break History On Theory And Testing

SPECIFIC AND GENERAL MENTAL ABILITIES

This study addresses concerns about general and special abilities. It also summarises early theories and tests mental capabilities. This review leaves out significant information. While some contributors are mentioned, it is important for readers to see them from the perspective of their contemporaries.

It is possible that the reader will want to consult other sources to gain a sense for each period's vocabulary or way of thinking. This review was organized primarily according to chronology.

Long-standing conjecture has been circulating about the nature human mental abilities. Aristotle, for example, distinguished between analytical and practical types of intelligence. (Tigner & Tigner2000). Bowman, 1989. (Doyle,

1974). The Chinese tests are part of a complex, over-time developed hiring system.

Bowman (1989), argues that discussions about ancient China's testing methods for mental abilities were precursors of many current issues in the field. These include the balance between memory, subject-matter competence, the impact of socio status on test results, and the application geographic quotas.

The Psychometric Strategy

Most stories about efforts to assess intelligence stem back to around the turn of 20th-century. Wundt's research was the catalyst for the development of experimental psychology (Mackintosh 2011). J. McKeen Cattell (Wundt's pupil) created an association testing system in which subjects were required to list as many words as possible within 20 seconds of hearing a single sound (Cattell & Bryant.1889).

Modern word fluency test have much in common with this approach. Cattell (1890) and Galton (1890), suggested a series tests to gauge mental ability.

They believed that the data collected by these activities on a wide population would reveal information about mental processes' consistency and interdependence. Cattell & Farrand (1896) recorded the observations made by Columbia University students over the years.

Wissler (1901), used Pearson's newly-created correlation method to analyze Cattell, Farrand's tests. Wissler (1901), page 1. "If a particular test is universal then its findings should match many other special testing." "And, in turn," said Wissler (1901 page 1).

He claimed that there wasn't any "significant" connection between the scores. However the definition of significant he used was not determined by probability but rather on how the word is used daily in speech. My calculations indicate that there is a 0.21 link between speed for letter cancellation and speed for color naming.

Wissler similarly described a correlation between the auditory-visual digit span of 0.39 to be substantial but modest. The most significant correlation between students' academic ranking and performance on mental assessments was in logical memories, at a r= 0.19.

Conversely, the correlations among students' relative ranking within different classes was significantly greater, with values of 0.60 to 0.75. Wissler's analysis revealed that Cattell&Farrand (1896), mental tests were not interdependent and are ineffective in real-world situations.

This study strongly opposed the utility of speeded reaction and perception tests for intelligence indicators. Wissler's assessment of the strength correlated was quite different from today.

Spearman (1904), suggested that mental tests should be subjected "correlational psychology". Spearman's correlation involved rank sorting data, contrary to Pearson's. This was done on three-sensory discrimination exams and three teacher assessed intellect assessments. Spearman (1903), discovering nine positive correlations among these measurements, concluded they all indicated a common factor.

He proposed a hierarchy separating the various types of intelligence. He proposed the hypothesis "intellective oneness". This hierarchy was arranged according to how general intelligence "saturated", each object. Each measure was seen to contain both general intelligence and an unrelated factor.

Spearman (1903):

Each branch of intellectual life shares one basic function (or set). However, the activity's remaining, more specialized parts seem to vary between branches.

Jensen(2000) explains that Spearman's concerns were primarily in theory and the composition of cognition. Spearman (1914), an older version of Spearman, developed a better approach to testing his two factors theory. It was applied to a larger number of Thorndike's mental exams. Spearman's method was used by Spearman to compute the tetrad discrepancies within the ratios that the pairs of correlations were among the four mental testing. If a single component causes correlations then the difference should not exceed the sampling error bounds.

Spearman (1914).

Two factors can determine the success of a group of neurons: the development and organization of those particular neurons and the overall state of cortex. The first can be called the "specific element" because it is unique for that particular performance. The "general" element is the one that is needed for every performance.

Spearman developed an elementary theory to explain the dependence of his two components on the physiology in the brain. Spearman created several methods to determine test score loadings on a single component (Vincent. 1953). Spearman might therefore be called the inventor single-factor analytical.

Thompson (1916), whose dice-throwing experiment showed that it could form intelligence's hierarchy without the need to have a general fact (g), disputed Spearman's claim. Thompson (1919) then conducted more simulations by using playing-cards. These simulations required Thompson (1919) to give values from dice or cards to create simulated test results.

Thompson's experiment was likely where the first Monte Carlo simulations were made of performance on mental tests. Thompson believed Spearman's support in general components was not necessary. It could be explained by many independent factors. This study is the first to suggest that Spearman's G might be a statistical artifact.

It's quite interesting to see the changes in Thompson and Spearman as they continue to debate about a general component. Deary, et.al. (2008) Spearman seems like to have accepted that in addition general and specific variables, there may be group-level factor (i.e. factors shared among a subset or tests).

Thompson, who is known to enjoy Spearman's type g, once said, "Surely, the true defense of g would be that it has proven beneficial" (Dearyet al.). Although historians can portray researchers as having fixed opinions, these perspectives, like many others, have changed throughout history.

Binet & Simon (1916), a British method, came up with a way to determine whether to send a child in a "special school" or keep them at home. They didn't make any assumptions about the prognosis and etiology of the child's situation. Instead they wanted to analyze the child. Binet & Simon were able to use more complex tasks that did not require laboratory experiments, which was a departure from the earlier Cattell & Galton (1890).

Binet & Simon (1916), stated that the scale that will be explained is "not a theoretical work; rather, it is based on long investigations." All of our tests have been repeatedly tested and those that did not hold up to testing were kept.

Binet & Simon were thus developed through empirical inquiry. Boake(2002) proved that the scale was valid because scores increased as you age and could identify children with mental impairments. Binet & Simon (1916), studied the character of traits that made "mental defectives different from other kids.

They believed that comprehension, reasoning, and thinking were all essential. However, they did not believe that memory was essential. An example of memory being insignificant is the case of a girl with exceptional memory who was "backward", which they now call a genius.

Boake (2002) said that Binet stressed how a test taken alone is of little significance, and that the critical data is included in a subject's average performance in several tests. Binet & Simon (1916), meanwhile noted that it was hard to determine which mental functions are being performed because they are numerous when discussing the test results.

Terman (1916), a translator and alterator of the Binet & Simon scalar, added new items and standardized the test on a large amount of kids, later translated and altered it. This scale was named the Stanford-Binet. Terman included questions to differentiate between children of different age and they were relevant in the overall scale.

Stanford-Binet's scale can appear to measure a single talent by adding elements that correspond with the overall score. Terman stated that a single test is insufficient as intelligence has many facets.

Terman (1916), suggested a range of uses for IQ test beyond spotting mental impairments. Terman (1918:page 165) states that his test "probes beneath schooling and provides a measure of basic brain capacity." Terman (1924), emphasized that mental tests are equally appropriate for experimental psychology and controlled trials over a long period of time. He observed that most experimental psychologists at the moment agreed with this view.

Based on variations of his "point" scale, Yerkes (1917), criticized the Binet- and Stamford–Binet-scales based on his. Yerkes stated that they should use tests to test fundamental psychological processes instead of differences across age groups. The psychological functions tests that Yerkes has developed can be used either individually or together. Yerkes further states that a particular test item should be relevant to all ages and produce a continuous result. The popularity scale for Yerkes points fell short of Terman and Binet.

Terman (1918), contributed in developing the tests that the US military used during the First World War. These scales were designed by a group led by Yerkes of well-known experimental psychologists. This group designed two tests: The Alpha, for those able to read and write English, as well as the Beta, for those who couldn't. The Alpha and the Beta army tests offered multiple choice questions.

According to Spring (1972), this was the criterion used to validate these tests. By comparing the test results to officer assessments of the soldier's worth as practical soldiers, Spring evaluated this skill. Spring concluded that this validation was similar in nature to Binet's evaluation of the suitability of youngsters for regular school instruction.

Spring explained that the army testing program and Simon's research assessed how people would perform under highly structured organizational structures. Kevles (1968), intelligence tests gained attention because they were not being given as much prior to the war.

Thorndike (1918), suggests that psychologists can reduce the infinite number and variety of inclinations of people to think, act and feel in particular ways to respond to various situations to just a few inclinations. These are known as traits or abilities or interests.

Thorndike stated in 1918, "If individuals are measured on a scale that is very roughly divided," their differences can be obscured. Thorndike (1918), explained that it is possible to have one type of individuals or as many as people.

Thorndike (1921), intelligence means the ability to make smart decisions. His opinion is that it would be foolish to try to separate intelligence from the emotional and vocational abilities of people. Thorndike also believed a person's aptitude could change depending upon their job. Thorndike believed test data were more valuable than their ability for predicting future performance.

Thorndike believes the test's content must be as close to the predicted skills as possible. Thorndike stated that the exams he took preferred words, numbers, spaces-forms, photographs, and ignored three-dimensional items and situations involving other people. This could be explained by convenience. Thorndike created several assessments that assessed specific skills and accomplishments related to subjects such as reading (Thorndike.1914a) and mathematics (19th century).

Thurstone (1934), states that Spearman's approach in tetrad differentiators often fails to show how only one factor can explain correlations within tests in a set of batteries. Thurstone (1934), stated in a statement that Spearman's theory is insufficient. While the proponent would dismiss the tests, the opponent would.

Thurstone believed that both conclusions are false and that the explanations of the relationships was not possible without more than one component. Thurstone (1934), said that we must recognize the multi-dimensionality within our minds before we can begin to isolate and describe specific skills. Thurstone used

Centroid to extract these multiple elements (Vincent, 1953).

Thurstone (1935), emphasized that this issue involves at most two components when discussing techniques to extract many elements. The first discusses the minimum variables required for intercorrelations to explain observed test scores.

The second involves the minimum number possible of factors needed to explain the correlations between test result results. The second problem concerns the rotation of components.

Thurstone (1935), says that the answer to the problem of an inexplicable amount of factor rotations can be found in the basic structure. This is because many factor loads are vanishingly tiny and result in a simple structure (i.e. the sparse matrix with factor loadings). Thurstone also devised techniques for higher level factor analysis.

Multiple component analysis was a tedious task that required a lot in manual labor. Thurstone & Thurstone (1941), praised the contributions of several assistants who helped with the computations. Thurstone & Thurstone (1941), based upon these techniques, identified verbal comprehend, word fluency. space, number and memorization as the six most important mental capacities that they considered to be indicative. They pointed out that perceptual Speed and deductive Reasoning were two additional mental skills they didn't as clearly identify.

Thurstone & Thurstone made the following observation:

No one knows the exact number. While only one memory factor is known at the moment, it is possible that there are many.

Raymond Cattell spotted many definitions in 1943 of intelligence in literature. He suggested that the adult mind could be thought of as a mixture of solid and malleable skills. Cattell's fluid intelligence includes the ability to identify relationships between things and distinguish them.

Crystallized Intelligence was used to establish the patterns earlier. After crystallizing intelligence, the fluid intelligence was no more necessary. In 1966, nine additional components were added to this hypothesis to account both cerebral prowess in addition to general personality traits (Horn & Cattell).

These nine characteristics relate to academic achievement and were fluid intelligence (or crystallized intelligence), imagery, speed, the use of concept labels, carefulness, clarity, and fluid intelligence. Horn & Cattell argued that the solution's nine elements were related and that this was due to interactions in the person's personal growth.

Cronbach & Meehl compiled in 1955 the findings from a committee appointed by the American Psychological Association to validate test items. As we mentioned earlier, test developers used different methods to choose test items.

The following criteria were used. It was crucial that construct validity included the emphasis on theory during the validation procedure.

Cronbach, Meehl (1955), define construct validation as a continuous process that validates tests but also supports them with evidence of validity. Cronbach (1957), encouraged the inclusion of experimental research within construct validation. Cronbach (1957), a noted that experimentalists were no longer considered to be independent of those who used correlational methods. Terman's time as an experimentalist was quite different to the present.

Cronbach (1957), suggested that collaboration between the fields could yield mutual benefits. It doesn't seem like this exchange happened at that time.

Kirk & McCarthy invented the Illinois Test of Psycholinguistic Abilities(ITPA) in 1961.

This tool is used to assess kids who are having difficulty in particular areas such as language, perception or behaviour. The belief was that children with learning difficulties have large skills differences, which leads to poor academic performance. Kirk (1968), believed that Stanford-Binet was insufficient for this task.

The ITPA contains nine subtests. These tests assess three functions- decoding/association and encoding-in each of two organizational levels' visual, auditory, and vocal channels. The ITPA was created as a way to test specific skills for children with learning difficulties. Elwood spoke out about automating psychological assessments back in 1969.

He suggested that automation could improve test item presentation and reliability as well as the validity and reliability of test results. It also might increase accuracy in recording and scoring answers, which would save time.

He showed details about an automated machine that could administer the majority of WAIS subscales. The results of this automated system were similar to manual testing. Elwood's device was made using antiquated technology, according to current standards. Despite technological advancements, computerized testing of mental ability is still very uncommon.

Carroll (1993), who re-factored correlation tables from extensive earlier research, did so by using a huge body of data. Carroll's method entails obliquely rotating initial correlation matrices. Higher-order factoring correlation matrices of the first-order elements, and sometimes the third. Based on these findings Carroll (1993), developed a three stratum theory, which included general, narrow and broad variables. Carroll considered Carroll's interpretations at each level to constitute the creation theory. The third and greatest strata level is called general intelligence (i.e. g).

The abilities of this second stratum include fluid intelligence, crystallized insight, memory and visual perception. Carroll explained that it is possible for more second-order components to be discovered.

Carroll (1993).

It is evident that all of the top names in psychometrics--Binet, Spearman, Thurstone, and Guilford, to mention a few--have had a deep interest in intelligence. All have admitted that developing theories of intelligence and cognition is a prerequisite for developing theories of intelligence.

Carroll also said that these pioneering thinkers relied more on common sense explanations rather than sophisticated cognitive theories in explaining behavior. Carroll spoke to many people about his mental faculties during several conversations.

One of these was whether g could be considered unitary in Kranzer & Jensen's

(1991). Kranzer & Jensen (1991), independent of any other "elementary cognitive actions" showed four main components that contributed to the prediction and estimation of g.

They concluded that, because the components were orthogonal they required g to have at minimum four parts. Kranzer & Jensen concluded with the support of Detterman's (1982), theory stating that intelligence is the sum a number of orthogonal variables.

Carroll (1991) said that Kranzer & Jensen (1991), only had an estimated for g. He offered hypothetical example factor matrices and suggested that it might be more cost-effective to assume a unitary g. Carroll (1994), Humphries (1994), and Carroll (1994), engaged in discussion about a behaviorist viewpoint of intelligence.

Humphries states that intelligence refers to the person's ability to use all of his or her intellectual knowledge at once. Humphries stated that intelligence is not just a mathematical dimension. Carroll

(1994), on the other hand, claimed that intelligence and cognitive traits were inherent to every person rather than learned skills.

The Neuropsychological Approach

Finger (1994), Democritus (c. 460-370 B.C. Galen (A.D. 120-200), who connected brain and intellect, believed that the head governs logical functions. A papyrus found in ancient Egypt shows that speech loss due to a head injury is related to speech loss (Sondhaus&Finger, 1988).

Broca's description a patient who had lost their ability speak due to a left inferior frontal cortical lesion was a very significant event in thinking about location of function. This led to modern neuropsychology (Finger, 1994).

Teuber (1955), proposed double dissociation to pinpoint a function's exact location. This technique employs two behavioral tests to show functional separation of two brain areas. Each test is affected in one area but not in the other.

This technique was later used by many neuropsychological researchers to describe the various types of brain injury that patients with brain damage suffer.

Shallice (1988), in a review of literature, suggested that double disociations exhibit functional specializations to sub-processes involved in perception and memory as well as speech and output systems. Double dissociation does have its critics. Plaut (1995), a synthetic connectionist network, found that it did not possess a modular framework for creating a twofold separation. Plaut says that these results challenge the theory of single-case investigations.

Milner (1957), Scoville (1957), and Milner (1957), provided examples of severe memories loss after the hippocampus was removed in order to cure uncontrollable Epilepsy. Both provided causal explanations for the patient's behavior and clearly distinguished between the Wechsler intelligence- and memory-scales to describe this memory decline. Toal

(1957), as well as others' research (Erickson & Scott 1976) questioned the Wechsler's suitability to describe organic memory issues.

Toal believes that the Wechsler scale for memory is based on a confusing "commonsense" memory concept. It leaves no clear indication about what it is measuring. Many studies have been conducted to analyze the characteristics amnesic impairments as well as pinpoint dissociable disorders. These findings led to the creation and revision of memory test batteries (e.g. Delise et.al., 1991) (Kent 2017.

Chase et al. (1984) studied the relationship between WAIS scores in Alzheimer's patients, and cerebral glucose metabolism in healthy individuals. According to their findings performance on the verbal test was related to activity within the left perisylvian. The performance subtest however was linked to activity within the right posterior paraietal. This study was groundbreaking in mapping brain regions to determine individual differences in mental skills. It used modern neuroimaging technologies.

There are also correlations between neuroimaging and cognitive task performance that have led to novel theories, such as the notion of greater mental efficiency when there is higher cognitive task completion (Deary & Carly, 1997).

Livingstone & Hubel (1987a), gave evidence that the monkeys' visual system could process form, color, motion, and depth independently. Livingstone & Hubel (1987a), showed that humans also have psychophysical evidence to support the notion of distinct processing channels for similar visual elements. They didn't examine any individual variations.

But, the hypothesis about distinct processing streams proved to have been very useful in directing neuroscientific research in the future to look at how information is processed by specialized networks. Reitan and other researchers had focused on rigid localizationist concerns. This led to a shift away. "Selectively distributed processing" could resolve the dispute between equipotentiality, localization of function, and both (Mesulam.1998).

Trends and Current Issues

Over time, different interpretations have been given to the history of ability-testing. Tyler (1965). Tyler states that intelligence was defined differently in early mental tests. This includes concepts like abstract thought, learning, judgment, and so on.

Tyler (1965), states that mental testing was primarily practical and prevented psychology from becoming too complicated. This point of view was in keeping with the time's pragmatic orientation that stressed performance prediction across many disciplines.

Carroll & Maxwell (1979),

There has always been a conflict between those that believe you can easily sum up human cognitive ability in one definition.

There is a conflict between those who think intelligence can be summed up in a single definition and those that prefer to emphasize its multidimensionality. Current research is based on a multifactorial view.

Recent research has highlighted the progressive nature and evolution of theory development within this field in several studies of the history in human mental talent research (e.g. Flanagan et.al. (2014); Schneider & Flanagan (2015)). This view is consistent in the growing interest of using individual characteristics to develop theories. The Cattell-Horn-Carroll Model (CHC), is very popular.

According to Schneider & Flanagan (2015)

The CHC Hypothesis is not so much a new theory as it is an extension of substantial discoveries made earlier by Spearman, Thurstone and other pioneering scholars.

Geisinger (1999) says psychological testing is still rapidly developing. Similarly, Riley et al. (2017) claim:

Every version of the Wechsler Adult Intelligence Scales (WAIS) and the Wechsler Intelligence Scale for Childrens (WISC), contains adjustments based primarily on new information published in both primary as applied literature.

Boake (2002) argues the contrary. While this popular IQ test underwent many changes, it remained essentially unchanged. He mentions several WAIS subscales before the Wechsler Bellevue was formed.

Boake (2012) claims that all Wechsler Bellevue Subtests, other than Block Design, were derived using Army tests. Since then, there has not been much change to the substance. Tulsky et.al.2003b states that the only change to the content was in the third revision's Symbol Search supplemental section test. Most modifications focused on new methods to compute index scores and revising standards.

Boake 2002 states:

The Wechsler-Bellevue Intelligence Scale (a collection of intelligence test) was created in the 1880s. The Wechsler test subtests are a result of the main cognitive evaluation methods used prior to World War I.

WAIS scales have therefore undergone significant interpretational changes rather than being changed in substance. Cronbach (1975) says that there has been "waxed, waned", public debate over the testing of mental talents since the invention of these tests. These debates touch the socioeconomic, racial, and immigrant variation in test results.

Cronbach (1975), suggests that this is due to journalists who tend to only report on the opposite side of an argument when writing about scholarly articles.

However, it is clear that psychologists may have made controversial public statements. This includes the book by Hernstein & Murray (1994), in which they discussed, among others, differences in intelligence between races.

Walsh et.al. stated that Galton Jackson Maudsley Spearman, Jackson, Maudsley, Maudsley, as well as Spearman, cited science to support the preservation of the status quo. (2014). Jensen, (2000) asserts Spearman believed that one could evaluate a person's eligibility for vote or to have children based only on the measurement and g.

Thurstone acknowledged that people can possess many different skills, but he also stated:

If the data support the gene explanation, biologists can not be accused as being undemocratic. Mother Nature must be undemocratic if any one is interested (Thurstone 1956).

According to Neisser et al. (1996) These topics pose a problem because there is uncertainty as to the source, nature and measurement of intelligence.

According to Neisser et al. (1996),

It is unacceptable that a topic with so many open problems and unanswered queries has been discussed in such a confident manner.

Chapter 2: What Are Mental Absilities?

(PRIMARY, SECONDARY AND SECONDARY TIME MENTAL ABILITIES

Definition of Mental Ability

Some examples of mental abilities include the ability learn, remember and comprehend information. You also need the attributes (capacity), ability and power to complete tasks.

General Mental Ability

"General mental abilities" (GMA) refers specifically to the ability of a person to comprehend directions and learn. Tests of general cognitive capacity include scales that evaluate specific constructs, including verbal, mechanical and numerical as well as social and spatial aptitude.

The score is the most important because it is more influential than specific abilities in determining performance variation.

General Mental Ability tests

A variety of cognitive abilities and traits are evaluated in general mental capacity tests.

Longer tests often measure the following characteristics.

* General knowledge: The level of information acquired by a person on a range of subjects. Long-term memory.

* Social intelligence: The ability to both verbally as well as visually to use norms that allow for moral and ethical judgments, in order to evaluate social behavior.

* Arithmetic (problem-solving and mathematical reasoning skills).

* Verbal thoughts: The ability classify, to understand similarities and contradictions, and to draw nuances in comparisons.

* Vocabulary. Extensive acquisition of linguistic notions. Demonstrates an ability to use information effectively, be receptive to information and communicate well.

* Coding - Flexibility and rapid learning.

* Orienting details is the ability to recognize key facts using perceptual as well as analytical abilities.

* Spatial rotation - Being able to see things in many dimensions and angles.

* Spatial reasoning refers to the ability understand an object's different components and how they interact.

Shorter Tests

Although there are other shorter tests that can be used to assess general mental capability, the Wonderlic Personnel Test (which lasts 12 minutes) is the most reliable. These include conceptual comparisons, word-sentence meanings, sequential logic, deductive thinking, sequential reasoning as well as detail matching, analysis, of geometric figures, story issues that require mathematical solution, and deductive and sequential logic.

The multi-choice test format is not the best. Test takers must fill in their responses to ensure that an extensive amount of data can be accessed for examination. Compare the candidate's test score with the minimum requirements for different occupational categories.

The Wonderlic Personnel Test provides quantitative insight into how adaptable and able to handle difficulties while working, the ease with which they can learn and whether they are likely to be satisfied with the job.

Higher scores are more likely than others to benefit from formal education and more likely will learn from on the job training. People with lower scores will need more instruction, practice and supervision.

Critical Thinking Test

Managers have to be objective about assessing the opinions and business proposals of their staff. Watson Glaser is a widely-used critical thinking assessment. It tests one's ability to use multiple forms of critical thought. To draw a conclusion from a collection of data.

* What unstated assumption exists?

* What can one infer about the conclusions relative truth or falsity of the conclusion?

* Does the evidence support the conclusion logically

* The relative merits or weaknesses of a particular claim and its conclusion

Can compare scores to occupational and management level comparables.

Types of Mental Abilities

Basic Mental Capabilities

* Memory Association: A person's ability for recall and memory.

* Numerical Capability: The ability for solving mathematical problems.

* Perceptual Speed is the ability to recognize similarities and differences between objects.

* Reasoning: Ability to find rules by reasoning

* Spatial vision: The ability spatially to visualize relationships.

Importance of Mental Abilities

A worker's functional capacity is dependent on their mental abilities, in particular a mental worker.

The mind uses mental abilities, also called psychological skills. It includes, among other skills, the ability build confidence, create goals, and use constructive self talk. You can increase your academic achievement and overall well being.

Categories for mental disabilities

There are 2 types of mental capabilities: Primary and Secondary.

Intelligence

Intelligence, if you take a closer look, is an amazing thing to measure. I was able to clearly recall the man's I.Q. while working for a county program. He seemed relatively normal and could maintain a conversation. After his I.Q. He was then tested for his I.Q.

The ability to acquire knowledge, apply it to solve challenges or find solutions is a broad definition of intelligence. Two factors influence my loose interpretation. The second, and most important, explanation is that it doesn't exist as a physical structure. Because it's a theoretical construct, it has been studied through psychological research, testing and the formulation of hypotheses regarding how information is processed. While it may seem easy to measure the object as a real one, it is more difficult than measuring your spleen's output and your skull's volume.

There is a difference between primary and secondary mental abilities. This second reason is why we are using a wide definition of intelligence. Both will require explanation. So let's each explain our part.

Primary Mental Conditions

L.L. L.L. Thurstone may have been described as a latent central construct, which can account virtually for all cognitive difference. Thurstone began research after disagreements between the two main camps were raised by intelligence tests. One group claimed intellect was only one type of intelligence. Others held that intellect has multiple dimensions and can display higher and lower levels.

Thurstone did numerous psychological tests. He discovered that intelligence manifests in limited ways. It's a bit confusing, since it seems like I'm contradicting two things. Thurstone discovered that only few factors are really relevant when assessing I.Q. Thurstone discovered that there are only a handful of factors that really matter when evaluating I.Q.

* Verbal understanding.

* Spatial orientation

* Using inductive logic

* Quantity facility

* Word fluidity

* Relational memories

* Perceptual speed

These are very difficult concepts to learn by yourself. Imagine you are trying to research associative and linguistic memory, but not also including language. Or, alternatively, how does one use numbers without requiring language? These fundamental mental abilities can also be affected or supported with additional factors.

To fully grasp the fundamentals of each, we must also examine secondary mental abilities.

Function Of Primary Mental Abilities

Primary mental abilities work in a similar way to Legos, or parts of an electronic erector set. You can't use just one Lego component or erector kit part to measure intelligence.

Secondary Mental Abilities

The dominant opinion is that secondary skills are derived form core talents and their overall clusters. This interaction with broad underlying themes is the norm.

Most research on intelligence/mental capacity shows that "intelligence" cannot be quantified or defined. However, specific mental abilities can help to identify a person's strengths, as well as their weaknesses.

Knowing the meaning of each cognitive assessment when considering secondary mental talents will help to better understand what the person is being asked for and will reveal which skills and ability are being utilized.

The two critical secondary mental capacities frequently mentioned in the literature include:

* Crystallized intelligence.

* Fluid intelligence.

Crystallized Intelligence:

Our ability demonstrate understanding, expressive thought, comprehension, and crystallized intelligence is usually evaluated using linguistic tools such as vocabulary and analogies.

The higher the score, the greater chance that an individual will be able combine knowledge in a very sophisticated manner.

Crystallized intelligence is typically influenced by someone's education level, life experiences, and culture.

Fluid Intelligence:

Fluid intelligence, in contrast to crystallized intellect, is less structured and knowledge-based. It's the ability to recognise linkages, understand patterns, predict the consequences, and make predictions about these relationships.

These skills include thinking, problem-solving, flexibility and intellectual flexibility. When presented with new scenarios and settings, fluid intelligence and fluid reasoning can be very useful.

Human fluid reasoning can be described as a process of trial and error that is independent of other constructions.

Primary mental abilities should be the most important guide for grouping second mental abilities. Many of these talents are evaluated using either implicitly and explicitly standardized IQ tests. As with IQ test results, it is important that you consider the impact of education, culture, age, or other variables on a person's ability. Research shows that secondary mental abilities can be affected by the life-span development process.

These skills are more susceptible to repetition and reinforcement.

Conclusion:

Our mental state affects our emotional, psychological and social well-being. It influences our thoughts and emotional responses as well. It affects how we respond to stress and how we interact with other people. Mental health is essential at all stages of life, from childhood and adolescence through adulthood.

Chapter 3: Spiritual Balance: What Is It? Does It Work, And

DOES IT HAVE A PLACE INSIDE MODERN HEALTHCARE?

This chapter will address the following points:

* Self-healing visualization

* My introduction on the healing

* The healing session

* Possible mechanisms to effect

* Evidence of effectiveness through research

* Its position in modern healthcare

Self-healing Visualization

To communicate my understanding about spiritual healing, which I believe is better experienced than explained, I decided to start by showing us how to do a self-healing visualization. It will give us a taste and boost our energy.

It is an excellent practice to encourage individuals and help them to help themselves when necessary. We often provide this transcript for people who come for healing.

The Introduction of My Healing

I thought that you might be interested to learn how I overcame complete doubt and began to heal. It was Christmas fifteen years back that my uncle, a gentle-mannered businessman and entrepreneur, revealed his plans to become healer. All of us felt shocked.

Although this seemed like biased reporting, he did tell me about his experiences in healing people. I was intrigued enough that I decided to explore more. After my uncle had given her the number, I called the Leeds healing tutor.

She started to talk with me about a healing intro course that she was offering. But, I cut her off to emphasize that while I wasn't interested being a healer, I was curious to know more. She advised me to enroll in the introductory course in three weeks. In the meantime, however, I might try to send healing, positive energy via me, my children or plants. I cannot believe that I'm doing it, I thought as i held my hands up in front the cactus plants in the kitchen. It was embarrassing.

I forgot all about healing until about two week before the course was due to start. I was feeling sick at 3 AM and was afraid that I would have no choice but to go to bed for my third night.

I chose to try the healing lark as I was so exhausted I couldn't stand it. I did not use the exact words. I was just exhausted and unmotivated.

I was shocked at what happened next: I felt a warmth around my chest, my fingertips began to tingle, I felt a blue light in me head, and I felt a warm band of heat. My gasping stopped abruptly. As you can imagine I was somewhat alarmed by the outcome and told my spouse the next day that it would be impossible for him to guess what had happened on the previous evening.

Because I was certain there was something to it, I listened.

I currently offer healing in three locations.

Let's begin with Leeds Healing Centre. Here, individuals can come to receive healing.

Second, the Positive Care Programme is an established charity that offers 24 week individual and small group complementary therapies and motivational workshops. Referrals to the Primary Care Mental Health Team, local charities and healthcare day centers for long-term patients and their caregivers. A large percentage of individuals suffer from level 1 or level 2 mental disorders.

Third is the York Association for the Care and Resettlement of Offenders. This group works to improve the energy of staff and ex-offenders.

A Definition of Healing

It involves the sending of energy from the healer into the patient. It encourages self healing through the relief of physical tension, relaxation and improvement of the immune system. Healing is natural and non-invasive. It aims at restoring equilibrium and overall wellness to the receiver (NFSH Healing Trust).

Spiritual healing is not possible without a solid faith. It is possible to heal even the most skeptical. It is therefore not faith healing.

Latin's "spiritus", meaning "breath of living water," is where "spiritual" derives its name. The spiritual aspect refers to energy from the spiritual realm that has profound effects on our spiritual selves. In other words, the healer taps into "Universal", or Divine energy to channel healing in the body, mind,, and spirit. During healing, energy will be transferred.

Components For Healing:

* If one has the right intentions, one can guide universal energy and spirit (in a spiritual sense).

* The aura (human-energy field) increases the "spiritual vibrations" of the human body by drawing attention to it.

* One can then develop his/her highest nature fully and improve one's overall health.

* Multiple treatments will be needed to overcome the body's inertia.

* When people are ill, it is not unusual for them to complain about their "poor energy". But when someone is healthy, they will say they have "bursting" energy.

People suffering from chronic diseases often need 6-8 sessions to make progress.

What Happens in The Therapy Session

* The recipient is seated on either a couch or a chair.

* Healing practitioners tap into the healing energy.

* Energy is directed around the body to promote healing (typically through the healer's hand).

You cannot guarantee any result. They cannot claim to be healers because they only serve as a conduit for healing energies. The healer can provide healing remotely even if they're not physically present. The healer uses visualization and attunement in this instance to promote the patient's well-being and self-healing.

Who Can We Help?

* Anyone. Healing helps to lessen unwanted energetic masses (such fear or anger) in many people.

* Commonly, people with mental or physical health conditions such as depression and anxiety, backache and arthritis, cancer, me and bipolar disorder are often "short on energies" and feel "outof their element."

What Happens to People During Healing?

A variety of feelings, best described by "flowing energy":

* Warmth from the healer's hand or general reassuring warmth

* Cold

* Tingling

* Other sensations like touch, movement, or surfacing of pain

Effects of Healing:

Although these events are usually very significant in the patient's life, they aren't always specific. e.g.

* Pain relief

* A more profound sense for calm and a lighter burden

* Relief of bodily ailments

* A sense that you are connected with the cosmos

* Vitality increase

Case Study

* David was a customer from the Leeds Healing Center. David's MIND support employee had recommended him to us. David arrived looking rather messy.

* Ten years' worth of worry and depression and little sleep.

* Taking antidepressants

* Taken a CBT training course

* At one end of his rope

* The client said that the first session was relaxing. However, the following week the client reported that he slept soundly for a long time.

* Attended regularly for 4 months. Then, approximately every 2 weeks for the subsequent 2 months.

* Feeled lighter, more at ease, as well as content

* Anxiety attacks have been stopped

* Stopping use of antidepressants (with consent from his GP).

* Currently trying to adjust to volunteering at a nearby charitable shop

What is the Healing Process?

Uncertainty surrounding the healing process is the biggest barrier to its acceptance in healthcare. Until there is a strong mechanism to heal, healing will still be dismissed as a placebo effect. This is something I do not believe to be the case. I'll show you.

I visualize healing when I channel it. A black cloud containing "bad" energy was visible surrounding the woman during her Leeds Healing Centre treatment. It was seen that the energy had escaped from her right-side top.

When I asked her about how the healing was going, she answered that she felt good. She also felt something pass through her skull. The woman spoke to me while another healer was listening and she revealed to me that the woman had seen the dark cloud appear on her head. It appears that all three of them felt the exact same vibe.

Laboratory tests have shown that healing works. These experiments support the idea that the healer can be used to channel energy. Electromagnetic research reveals "extraordinarily vast"

Low-frequency magnetic forces will be recorded in healers' hands. To speed up the healing process, they require low frequencies (such as those in various forms of electrotherapy).

It was found that patients' brain waves shift in healing sessions to synchronize themselves with their healer. Electroencephalograms have shown enhanced alpha brain waves within the healer. Numerous studies have confirmed remote EEG connectivity. Regardless of the actions taken by the healer, the patient seems capable of receiving it.

Distant Intentional Connection's use of functional resonance image (fMRI), suggests that distant healing is being promoted by the experiment.

* "Sending thoughts from afar" is the definition and practice of distant intention.

* A distant intention healing, which was unknown to the recipient, was transmitted at intervals over two minutes (in sensory isolation of the healer).

* Extremely statistically meaningful differences between control and sent (no-send) during activation of certain brain functions by the recipient

The evidence is there that people can be healed and redeemed. What is the best part about it?

Oschman has an idea for a mechanism. Oschman is imagining a mechanism that would allow animals to extend into the cell plasma. This creates a continuum of electromagnetic energy and connects all cells. The body works because every component communicates instantly and continuously with the other (20 times faster as the central nervous sistem). (The theory of chemical communication through synapses may be too slow.

He believes that the optimal magnetic flow is dependent on a cohesive environment and a strong body. The aura is the extension of electromagnetic energy to the body's natural world. People can receive healing vibrations or intentions when they interact with the outer world.

Undoubtedly, many people can "know", after entering a room, if there was a fight. Bad energy can be detected in our aura. No matter what anyone says or does, we will always be able to tell if they have good or poor intentions.

To be able to heal, it may be necessary to reexamine reality. The quantum nature in which all things are interconnected is now known, but is no longer believed to exist. Thus, long after their first interaction-- possibly at the instant of the "Big Bang"-- two objects remain connected via time and space without exchanging conventional communication. Einstein referred to this connection as "spooky actions at a far"

Einstein's Special Theory of Relativity claims that matter (atoms and photons) is two sides of a single coin. Dean Radin also believes that bioelectromagnetic waves around our bodies can be entangled with electromagnetic field within our immediate environment, and with photons or energy from the rest the universe. He proposed that reality is connected through an entangled fabric.

Another possibility is the holographic realm, in which the universe could be a 3-D projected image from a Tier of Reality that exists independently from your time and place, despite it appearing to be manufactured from material objects.

This idea was separately developed by Karl Pribram, neurophysiologist, and David Bohm who is a physicist. Bohm was Einstein's mentor and a famous quantum physicist. Bohm was an independent thinker, as were Pribram. Their theories helped to clarify many phenomena not only in neurophysiological science but also in eerie and mystical realms. This paradigm is used mathematically by scientists who study and analyze the universe.

Michael Talbot wants to know if the mystics' assertions that reality is an ethereal symphony resonant wave pattern and not an illusion, known as "Maya", are accurate. Is this a "frequency realm" that transforms into reality as we know and understand it?

John von Neuman and Henry Stapp both concur. Both John von Neuman and Henry Stapp agree that the conscious is responsible for dispersing concurrent virtual states into one unified awareness state. This raises the possibility of another person's thoughts and brain affecting an item, a person or other human organs.

Probabilistic brain states tend to preferentially go into specific states. This could be how healing intentions make an impression. It is hard to grasp the fundamental workings of something so ethereal like healing.

But, I prefer this declaration from T. H. Huxley the English biologist.

You can approach facts by following the advice of "Sit before truth like a little boy, and be willing to give up all preconceived ideas, follow humbly wherever and whenever Nature leads."

He says that I am too skeptical about dismissing any possibility of something. Jack Angelo said the following regarding the method of healing:

Spiritual healing is based around the notion that everyone is interconnected on an "energetic" level. This concept is now supported by natural philosophy. It is believed that healing may affect the harmony of the mind, the body, and the spirit through stimulating thought at an active level.

The NHS's acceptance of healing is crucial for its legitimacy. The key to healing is knowledge. The patient's perspective is crucial. It is not about the method but the positive outcomes that are important. In the same way, I can speak with my friend via Skype from abroad as if she were near me.

Research is proving the effectiveness of spiritual healing

Jonas or Crawford list at least 2200 published studies regarding spiritual healing and prayer, energy medicine, healing with intention, and remote healing. However, many use subpar techniques. A lot of people don't feel any benefits after multiple healing sessions. This is based on anecdotal evidence and healers. According to NFSH Healing Trust:

It is very rare for healing to not be positive in some way.

Only a handful of people notice an immediate effect. Many clients feel their despair disappear or their chronic suffering vanish after the initial healing session. A few people don't benefit from the process of healing. It is possible that some of these individuals don't want to relinquish their sick person status because they have a stake.

A survey of people who support complementary therapies but don't necessarily believe in healing has shown:

* 87% (92/106) of those who felt healing had benefitted them agreed to or strongly agreed.

* 12% (13/106) said they were "unsure". (Most only attended one or a few sessions.)

* One person voiced their disagreement.

Dan Benor, the first scientist to treat healing as a scientific matter, was it. He conducted controlled experiments in 155 subjects, including enzymes, microorganisms and cells from plants, animals, and people. Half of them produced statistically significant data supporting the healing effect. He discovered that there isn't much research to support the healing effect of human illness.

There have been two reviews on human healing randomized controlled trials (RCTs). Nearly half of the trials showed statistically significant variations from controls.

* Neil Abbott reviewed ten of 22 publications. They all had a significant impact upon healing.

* The Astin Harkness, Ernst and Ernst reviewed 23 trials involving 2,774 subjects. Thirteen of the 57 percent of trials showed statistically significant effects. Nine trials were not different from control groups, while one trial revealed a detrimental effect.

However, most trials had poor design and methodology. Many also had biased reporting.

In an RCT, which looked at the impact spiritual healing on chronic or acute pain (which was the primary outcome), there was no statistically significant improvement in pain. It did show significant differences from the control in terms of both non-specific, large effects and psychological benefits.

However, there were many criticisms of the trial, including for its design. The impact size was considered too small for chronic pain. These non-specific symptoms included "changes" in discomfort and "strange" sensations (such as seeing light or colors) that were noted. These complicated results were accepted as part of healing folklore.

Research methods should be focused on the goal of healing. Not just to restore health and relieve symptoms, but to also help people heal themselves within a holistic perspective of their own health.

This is essential to avoid an incorrect evaluation when investigating spiritual healing. This is something that most reductionist research methodologies don't consider. The healer (X), for example, placed her hand on a woman's back.

When X (the healing practitioner) touched my back, I thought about the horrible things that had happened in the recent past. I was able to realize that this was not a part anymore of me, and that I could let the past go. I have to get up.

She had been seeking healing to ease her back pain. I would not have noticed the "non-specific effects" of the healing during a trial looking at pain relief. Randomized controlled trials are required to overcome many methodological problems in order to determine the effectiveness or spiritual healing.

First, sampling can be problematic.

* Generalizability. The patients chosen to be part of a trial may have different belief systems and coping methods than the

usual patients who come for healing. This could impact the treatment outcome. Traditional medical care is generally distinct from the administration or healing.

* Therapeutic Expectation. If there is an expectation of therapeutic benefits due to faith and healing, results in nonblinded trials may be skewed.

* Wide ranges of symptoms: People who seek healing might be seeking it for reasons other than a medical condition. Studies on the efficacy or healing of a particular condition may not apply.

Second, there may be problems with the trial.

* Standardization. The practitioner will often be explicitly acknowledged in the treatment. This may make standardization of treatment within trials a problem. It requires, for instance, stratification of individual healers in randomization.

* Practitioner influence and user influence: The healing action aims to

increase the patient's entire healing process and goes beyond a mere collection of skills. It might be difficult to keep human experience at the core of reductionist scientific analysis.

* Controls Blinding isn't always an option. Instead pragmatic trials using standard medical attention as the control will be required.

* Recognizing Healing: What Components Help in Healing? Is it the intention of healing, the energy channeling and the users' expectations or the relationship with a healer? These are all critical.

Third, the measurement of outcomes may have issues.

* Measurable outcomes: Not all healings can be measured. The selection of RCT end measurements can significantly affect efficacy assessments.

* The illness role: Some ideologies claim that diseases are a manifestation of a balancing issue. Many people know someone who gets a bad cold or backache

when they're worried. It is necessary to record the lives of people after they have received treatment and any subsequent improvements in their health.

* Chronic illness. Because long-term patients with chronic illnesses often have a relapsing/remitting disease pattern, change is usually gradual and subtle. There may be other factors that cause the effects reported.

* There are variations in experience. One person may find treatment immediately and another might take a few more weeks. These variables should be considered in trial design. The trick is to combine complementary therapists' philosophical concerns, with rigorous methodological demands.

Modern Healthcare: Healing and Healing

The House of Lords Select Committee on Science and Technology spoke with many industry experts and researched alternative and complementary medicine and its use for healthcare.

The report on complementary, alternative and medicine classified healing as a group 2 therapy. This is due to the fact that it is a supplement and not a cure-all.

Spiritual healing has become an increasingly common alternative therapy.

* There have been over 14,000 healing practitioners registered by primary healing organizations.

* Physicians often recommend healers to patients.

* The NHS (GPs offices, oncology unit, hospices, mental health hospitals, and hospices) use it.

* The UK has NFSH Healing Trust Healing Centers.

* NHS healers can work as volunteers, or sometimes as employees. This is rare, however.

If modern healing is to be solidified within healthcare, then we need better research, good training for healers, and high standards of professional practice.

For the following reasons you might want contact the NFSH Healing Trust. For patients who need healing, you can call the NFSH Healing Trust (Charity No. 1094702)

* It is the UK's oldest and largest membership organization for Spiritual Healers.

* It is certified by instructors and trained to national standards.

* The minimum time for training is two years. The final exam meets national requirements and emphasizes the healer's personal development.

* It is covered in professional insurance, a process of discipline, and a code to conduct for professionals.

* The UK has more than 50 Healing and Rehabilitation Centers that are managed by volunteers.

My talk led to the NFSH Healing Trust offering a new member course for nurses/medical workers. This course is four days in duration due to prior learning. Next is mentoring a seasoned healing practitioner member for at minimum 12 months.

Visualization To Enhance Energetic Vibrations

This can be done sitting or standing.

By focusing on your feet and the Earth, you can ground yourself. The energy transfer between your feet below and the ground is obvious at this moment. Feel the support and love of the Earth.

Now, turn your attention inward towards the energy or lightbulb which makes up your true self or Soul, or life force. Don't worry if this isn't something you can "see". All you need to know is that it is there.

Now turn your attention upwards to the cosmos until it becomes clear that you can see or sense the Divine Light. This Divine Light is the source for all joy, serenity and unconditional love. Keep on focusing on fusing that Light into your life force. As the

71

Divine Energy descends on your body, allow this connection. This powerful Divine force is entering your soul, strengthening it, and giving it a sense of wholeness.

Allow this Light, to shine outwards, filling all cells in your body and nurturing them with healing and joy.

Imagine the Light expanding more. Think about it reaching an arm's distance from you on all sides. Imagine the empowering Light surrounding you, filling up to form a protective sphere. It is vitality, love, peace, and energizing.

You will feel the Earth connection if you return your attention to the bottoms. Feel calm and grounded. Your energy level is now appropriate for daily tasks. Next, close your eyes.

This visualization can raise your energy frequencies to receive Divine Light from the inside, making it a potent, healing visual. This visualization is a powerful and healing practice that you can continue to do throughout your day.

Chapter 4: What Is Telepathy And

How To Practise Elepathy

Do you remember thinking of someone and getting a text? It could be that you telepathically sent them a message instead of just a coincidence.

Frederic W. H. Myers (1882) was the first person to use the term "telepathy". Although many people still believe it to be pseudoscience, some research has proven that it can be used.

But what is telepathy and how can it be applied to your life? Telepathy experts are available to help you learn more and understand how to implement telepathy into your everyday life.

Telepathy is also called:

* Mental Surfing

* Mind Induction

* Telepath Physiology

* Telepathic Abilities/Powers

* Thought-Casting

What is Telepathy, and how can it help you?

The dictionary defines telepathy as "the ability to communicate ideas and/or thought through other than the five senses that children learn in school-seeing/hearing, tasting, tasting, and touching". Davida Raport, psychic andclairvoyant, believes that telepathy is a form or nonverbal communication.

"One person thinks or feels like transmitting concepts to another person," claims the author.

This is how she contacted you the next morning when she was thinking about you randomly as a college supporter. Or maybe your cousin called you and said, "OMG.

Capabilities

Information is often transferred between users using mental channels. These abilities, which are consistent with the concept of telepathy in its core, make them telepathy. However, there are many other mind-based talents that can also be used for telepathy. Common telepathic abilities include the ability read others' thoughts at will and to sense the presence in other minds using E.S.P.

Telepathy: Why do you need it?

Telepathy can prove to be very helpful if you are unable to speak or find the right words. You may be worried about being ignored, or even rejected. Even though you don't feel comfortable calling your ex for support, you feel the need to let them know your feelings.

Mystic Mystic, an aura reader and podcaster, stated that it's not always possible for us to express the things we wish to say to another person in our corporeal lives. It is possible to bring these messages forward by telepathically allowing the higher selves or soul identities to participate. It is possible to resolve issues that can't be accomplished face-to-face, like deep connections, forgiveness, or closure.

Andrea Donnelly, a celestial mentor/energy healer, advises you to consider telepathy as a natural extension your human talents if it feels like you're going wrong, anxious, stupid or unsure.

She recalls that my family used the term "small voices" to refer to it. I think it's helpful to see it as a sixth or other language you were born speaking and that you only need to recall. You can communicate with anyone and everything, including plants, animals, stars, through it. It acts like a psychic network.

Donnelly claims that you will become more aware of telepathy and accept it as a reality. Telepathy can change your life and relationships in a big way.

Telepathy:

Telepathy is a beautiful skill that everyone can use or practice. Rappaport believes that everyone can communicate thoughts, ideas, and feelings to other people, but only a few people are aware or actively using this skill. Like any skill or gift, practice is essential.

We asked experts to recommend that you first test your ability to telepathize with a friend, family member or other person. Why? Telepathically speaking with someone on a level you are already conversing with is more likely than not (even though you may not be aware of it). Mystic Michaela says that telepathy operates best when there's a connection or bond you have with someone. It is crucial to be aware of the telepathy you have with the people around.

1. Be in a Meditative State.

She suggests you to imagine the person you are trying to connect with standing or sitting in front of your face while you sit in meditation. Sending them love, gratitude and urgency is a good idea. It is possible to send emotion to them.

2. Informally communicate with someone you are concerned about.

Mystic Michaela suggests asking your higher self to "visit", and then delivering a message to strengthen a dream's telepathic connection, before you go to bed. "Speak to someone by your thoughts and emotional state. "Ask them to confirm that you received the message they sent," she states.

3. Always be ready for feedback.

Mystic Michaela will amaze you with the percentage of calls and texts that you receive over the next 24 hours. They could ask how many they've been trying to figure out about you or why you feel so compelled. She states that they may ask you at any given moment if you'd like anything or if things are going well. Contacting someone who isn't part of your life can be less active. She says they could DM you to say hello or share a post on social networks.

4. Be Patient.

Rappaport stresses that patience is a must when using telepathy. "Getting proficient in it will take time. It will be like mastering another skill. Repetition is important because thoughts can be strong. Some people are better at sending than others, but some may be better at receiving. They may be equally adept in both.

5. Consider a Mentor in Psychic Studies.

Donnelly urges you to maintain good spiritual hygiene. This is a way to ensure that your psychological development continues. As Donnelly said, this is often a reason why programs are important and why advisors and coaches can be invaluable.

"With Love, of course you want to be open to receiving things from the collective, such as ideas, worries and thoughts. Finding a mentor can help you get better at this.

Telepathy exercises

Ask Your Partner To Bring An Item From The Shop.

Rappaport suggests an easy experiment that you can do next time your friend makes late-night trips to the grocery store. Rappaport suggests another simple experiment. You'll be able to see them doing this. Next, let that go," she stated. If it worked you would quickly find that your partner purchased your favorite snack. If it didn't, you might try again.

Send an impression to a dearest.

Donnelly suggests performing the same activity with a buddy/partner instead of doing it individually. First, Donnelly recommends that you be quiet and contemplate the person. Then, it is time to communicate with them. Next, try to visualize a specific image (like a teddy) and wait to tell your spouse until then. Next, ask that your spouse or friend receive what you're sending.

Donnelly predicts folks will notice qualities such as "softness," child comfort, or plush. It wouldn't be literal, and it would require you to do this in order to understand how telepathy works.

Locate the Caller's Name.

As an additional practice, she advises tapping into that person asking. "All of us have displayed. But when the phone rings feel into it to determine if you recognize who it is. You will be more successful if you try out things and practice.

Mystic Michaela advises to always inquire for confirmation from the recipient in order to verify verification faster. She asserts that it will be easier to get a confirmation from the recipient if they are in tune with higher selves.

Telepathy Benefits:

Donnelly believes that telepathy will help you to see more meaningful patterns in your everyday life. According to Donnelly you will begin to recognize that everything happens with and for your benefit, not against you. Even the most disturbing of things become a beautiful tapestry.

She continued, "You will find that you take less responsibility for the actions and decisions of others and begin to see how we are achieving harmony with one another and the Earth." Instead of viewing life as a collection of accidental occurrences, it is important to understand that they are not random. When we are going through externally turbulent times, "It might be a gift" and a method of communication that can help us keep calm and focus.

Mystic Michaela believes Telepathy might be a good tool for friends or couples. As an example, let's suppose that you haven't heard back from your disciple in some time. Instead of expecting her to be upset with you you send her this message to let she know you're thinking about her.

It's important to connect with someone who can understand your emotions. Or what's taking place without you ever having the need to say a single word. Soon, when someone is in your neighborhood, you'll be capable of spotting them.

Telepathy's Negative Effects:

Mystic micha and Donnelly agreed that sharing and receiving so much information can be stressful. Donnelly suggests that people should be aware of their own boundaries as well as those of others. While it might seem tempting, invading someone's privacy is never a good idea. Prying is also unethical. You won't receive any information you don't need, but it's important to navigate psychic territory with honor.

Mystic Mystic, Michaela says that there are instances when you don't want to hear psychic signals from others. "Unfortunately though, toxic people are adept at manipulating our psychic connections to communicate with us negatively and grabbing our energy," Michaela said.

Mystic Michaela said that when you're in a bad mood, it's easy to feel lost or guilty. She also suggests that you think of reasons to try to help them. To manage relationships and strengthen bonds, it is essential that we are aware of telepathy within ourselves and others.

Learning telepathy takes time. Keep at it. Maybe your lover will bring home your favourite snack without you ever having to touch them.

Telepathy In Psychology

Psychotelepathy, in general, may be thought to be an energy transmission. If science interests you, it is important to be able to recognize the frequencies and energies in our environment. In the same way, the material body has the ability to exchange various frequencies. Telepathic contact may be possible when the frequencies of the other person match their vibrational range. Their psychic abilities allow them to communicate with divine energy. Telepathy is a form of parapsychology (ESP), although it may not be true science. It could also be a part of psychic systems.

I hope that you are now more open to telepathy. Let's go on and find out more about the many types of telepathy.

Types of Telepathic Ability

There are six primary forms of telepathy in the psychic space.

1. Telepathy latent:

It prevents telepathy from happening and is the ability to receive information with a delay. There is a slight delay between information sent and received during this good form of telepathy.

2. Retrocognitive Telepathy

This psychic ability lets one ask questions about someone's past. This is invaluable for psychics who are interested in understanding why certain events are happening right now.

3. Precognitive Telepathy

One who has this ability can see into the future.

4. Instinctual Telepathy

The way that your gut feels can help you learn about current circumstances.

5. Emotive Telepathy

The focus of the telepathic abilities described above is information or words. This psychic ability, however, is about emotions. It is possible for psychics to control their emotions and have influence.

6. Telepathy Superconscious:

You can use the power of your subconscious to get even the most obscure insights.

Telepathy Superpowers Are Real

It is difficult to observe or quantify this psychic skill, so it is often viewed as a fictitious type of communication. Believers claim that telepathy exists, just like electricity or gravity. Telepathy is not a new phenomena. You'll be amazed at the fact that everyone has the ability to telepathy. Telepathy has been around for centuries.

It can establish a connection with another person far away through psychic abilities. One can do many tasks using psychic abilities.

* Reading: You can feel or hear thoughts from another person using telepathy.

* Communication: Make contact with others using actions and words only.

* Impression. The psychic telepathy can help to implant an image, a concept, or message into another person's brain.

* Control: Telepathic communication could influence or direct another person's actions or thoughts.

Telepathy cannot be considered a spiritual phenomenon. In fact, there is strong correlation between science and psychology and the development telepathy.

Final Thoughts

Here are the basics of telepathy and spiritual-telepathy. Do you want information on psychic abilities like telepathy? Astro's experienced astrologers offer psychic readings that can help alleviate your doubts. They can also help with your search for a happy life.

Chapter 5: Aura & Aura Ready

WHAT THEY EXPECT AND WHAT TO LOOK FOR IN A READING

Are you intrigued at the fascinating world of aura readings, which can reveal a lot about your personality? Here's how to interpret your aura and the appeal it has to spiritual communities.

What is An Aura and Why Does it Matter?

A person's aura can be described as an electromagnetic field that surrounds them and is linked to their energy. However, not everyone can "see" it. A vibe check is a reading of your aura. Auras can spread. This helps explain why you may feel happier around people who are happy and positive, and why you feel exhausted around people who are unhappy.

The dictionary describes the aura, which is "an invisible electromagnetic field or energy field that surrounds all living organisms," as "an invisible emission or energy fields." An energy field can also surround inanimate objects or those created by humans. Contrary to the aura, which serves to guide the physical body and is fed by the heart (the main electrical generator of the body), these energy fields are thought to originate from the object. The energies that flow through the aura reflect our personalities and thoughts.

Function of The Aura

Your aura acts as a shield against the negative energies of your environment. Your aura is a link to the energies in your environment (it acts like an antenna or bridge).

The aura connects these energy centers with the chakras. This further processes them and often results in nerve, hormonal, and vascular activity.

Your aura sends signals that give information about you, and draws particular energies to yourself. The aura contains many interconnected parts that hold blueprints of your body, emotions consciousness, relationships, and personal growth.

What are the Seven Layers in The Aura?

The seven primary Chakras are located in the physical and emotional bodies, but they also exist in every layer in the aura. Each level is connected to the chakra, and the energy vibrates faster. Each layer corresponds to the Chakra denoted by the exact same number

Grace says that your aura consists of seven layers called auric layers. These are also known as bodies or plans. Each layer stands for a distinct concept. Imagine them as the layers inside an onion, with your actual body in the middle.

1. The Physical Aura Map:

The layer that signifies our bodily health and well-being is the physical aura. It is the skin's outermost level. Also known as "the ethereal" plane.

2. Emotional Aura Planner:

The emotional aura represents the plane to whom your emotions correspond. If your emotional level is high, this plane will indicate it. It will display your emotions and change color based on what you're feeling. If you're stressed, the plane may turn duller or smear.

3. Mental Aura Planning:

This plane deals with logic, cognition, reasoning. It is your third layer to the exterior.

4. Astral Body and Aura Plane

This plane is concerned in spiritual well-being and its movement outward. There you also store your love potential.

5. Etheric ura plane:

This plane holds your psychic powers. A transparent etheric etheric is a great way to connect and tap into the energy of others on your wavelength.

6. Celestial Ura Plane

Your intuition and dreams will be kept on this plane. It is the level to which you have reached enlightenment. Many people who possess a solid aura of heaven are very creative.

7. Causal Aura Plane:

This is your last aura plane. It helps you to balance all of the layers and provides a map for your future.

What does each color signify?

Your aura's hues is represented by one of the seven major chakras --the root and sacral, sun plexus, throat, heart, throat, middle, third eye, crown, and solar plexus. These chakras link to your aura (the aforementioned auric layers).

Understanding the chakra colors will help you to understand your aura.

Red:

Red makes your root chakra vibrate. Grace said that the root chakra is located at or near the base of your spine. It houses your core concerns. Once you have read your aura, it is essentially a foundation.

Orange:

The color orange is associated with your sacral, located in the lower abdomen. Grace says it contains the initial energy body, creativity, the ability to communicate with people and sexual energy.

Orange signifies that you can curl up under a blanket and feel secure. You're realistic and self-sufficient.

Yellow:

The color yellow is associated with your solar plexus chakra. This chakra is located just above your belly button.

Grace states it "holds the emotions, identity of your personal strength and personality." It defines your identity to others and to yourself. A yellow aura signifies that you're imaginative, curious and upbeat.

Green:

The color "green" is the representation of the center of the human heart. It symbolizes the energy that represents growth, healing, compassion, and transformation. Many have green auras. This includes teachers, parents and healers.

Pink:

Pink auras, while rare, share many similarities with the general green vibe. They are kind, compassionate, and genuinely love. A pink aura signifies that there is a lot more love and compassion than you are.

Blue:

The throat chakra is represented with the light hue of blue. It is all related to expression, self-expression and speaking one's truth. The dark blue color is used to represent the third chakra, which is associated mental clarity, intuition, and inward-focus.

Purple:

This color symbolizes the crown chakra. A purple aura represents compassion, empathy and the ability for magic and unusual energy to manifest. However, purple can indicate the need to rest or recuperate in an aura.

Violet:

You are creative and innovative. Most likely you attended a college of liberal arts. You live in the sky and often fall into daydreams. You have an excellent sense of intuition. Your friends and family admire your ability to see the bigger picture and your empathy.

Brown:

The aura's colors are dominated by browns, tans, and browns. They are driven by what they do and love manual labor. You're more pragmatic than purples. You are aware of the importance of planning and perseverance in achieving your goals.

Magenta:

If your aura is more magenta you will be independent. You're creative and witty so you have millions of TikTok fans. You're more inclined to create trends than follow them. While some may find your eccentricity odd, others secretly love your uniqueness. You are an exceptional person.

White:

White auras seem rare. This color resonates with the crown chakra, which is just above your head. Grace claims that it induces a sense and awareness of Oneness, All That IS, and our interconnectedness.

Black:

Your aura might be dark if it is filled with negative thoughts or emotions. This could hinder the flow and energy of your chakras.

The Best Places to Get Aura Reading

If you live outside of a major city, an aura reader may be able read your energy and provide you with a summary. Aura photography, which can be done for a very low price, is another popular way to see your aura.

AURLA, Aura & Energy and Aura & Energy offer virtual readings that are free if there isn't an aura studio near you.

How to read your aura.

Grace states that you can also use meditation to visualise your aura.

You can also see if there are any colors that form by moving your hands slowly, purposefully apart, and back together. To create friction, you can rub them together.

Once you're comfortable reading auras, you might also try it.

How to Read An Aura Image

Christina Lonsdale uses Polaroid to capture the radiant energy and creativity of others. She realized quickly that each image contained a different aspect about the subject.

These are the essentials:

* Photo Top. The space above you head is where your mental state and what's happening right now.

* Photo Left. The color in your lower left corner represents the inner state of your personality and persona. This is what you choose to reveal to your closest family members and friends.

* Photo Right: This will show your public identity or who it appears to be.

* The arch: This symbolizes your aspirations, or your ideals.

Lonsdale states that we are dealing with layers of ourselves here -- the intricacies, self -- which is what he finds so rewarding.

What to expect from an aura read.

Grace has been able to help customers leave readings. She is "astonishing in her insight and clarity to grasp their situation, including any life lessons or obstacles." My aura has been photographed before. After being stationary for around 20 second, I was able to photograph my aura using a Polaroid.

It was mainly crimson and a little bit of pink. This was what my reader considered self-assured. This felt 100% accurate, since I had recently ended my long-term relationship that was unhealthy for me.

Aura Photography and Aura Readings: What the Difference?

Aura readings and photos are two examples of spiritual practices that aim to improve self awareness. But, they can be experienced in different ways.

Mystic, Michaela, a reader of auras and author, The Angel Numbers Book's author, identifies growth potential for her readers. According to the author, "Reading an aura is a journey, where I take someone on the hand and show them all that needs love, that require more development, and that are waiting to heal."

Lonsdale argues that aura images can be enhanced if there's a tangible object to reference. She said you might also think about it, and possibly share it with other people.

When should your Aura be checked?

How often should your aura appear on camera? Lonsdale says it depends on the nature of your curiosity and what's happening in your life. "I've photographed many people before and most recommend that you have a time limit. However, I believe that it is better to be spontaneous than this.

A birthday review can be meaningful if it is requested. It is more effective to do some personal work and be more consistent whenever you notice a shift.

Aura readings indicate the same. It all comes down essentially to what Michaela believes is right in her gut. The author warns that while reading can be a good way to learn, it is not a good idea to read too often. "All solutions are already within your reach; they are all there for you.

Do the colors of you aura change with time?

People's aura colors can alter over time. Your aura's color changes throughout your life due to changes in your energetic energy. If you have a dominant aura color, you can find out more about its meaning and how to counteract it by reading about it.

Aura reader Rachelle Terter says that people with purple auras are more sensitive, intuitive, and introverted. Therefore, they need to learn how to set boundaries to prevent them from picking up negative energy. As a result, their auras will gradually lose their propensity to love purple.

Is it not what you want? Here are the steps to cleaning your aura.

There are many things you could do to boost your energy. Grace suggests that you can bathe in the sun or swim (especially if it's very cold). Smudging and sagging can be done by Grace. She also suggests that she engage in sound therapy, chakra-balancing meditations, and clothing for the aura you desire.

A personalized reading can provide you with additional guidance. You can also request some tips to help balance, clear, and enhance your chakras.

The bottom line.

All living things possess invisible energy fields known as auras. They can interpret your personality, biases or patterns using their hues. You can learn how your aura is read on your own, or have it read to you in person.

If you aren't satisfied with your aura's colors, you can change them over time through energy cleansing such as chakra work, sound therapy or meditation.

Chapter 6: Psychic Bilities &

Intuition

PSYCHIC DEVELOPMENT COURSE

Introduction

If you spend much time in Pagan, metaphysical or Pagan societies, you're bound to come across people with quite evident psychic abilities. Many people believe that every person has some degree of psychic ability. Some people display their abilities more clearly, while others conceal them beneath the surface.

Your own psychic-leaning and intuitive skills are probably yours, regardless how you view psychics and their abilities. One expert claimed that everyone had a gift for seeing the supernatural. We only need to learn how to develop our psychic powers.

This is because the term "psychic," as Laura Lynne Jackson, psychic medium, explains in Signs: The Secret Language of the Universe explains, can be interchangeably used with the word "intuitive." Your ability to perceive information outside the cognitive domain through your powers, is known as your ability "psychic," according to the speaker. It can happen both consciously and unconsciously.

Need persuasion? Are you a victim of someone looking at you and turning away? Maybe you had a flash of insight about someone. Then you met them later in life. Or maybe you felt something terrible when you entered the space. All these are examples of intuitive psychic ability.

What Does Psychic Actually Mean?

Webster's New World Dictionary defines psychological as:

* Concerning, or involving, the psyche and mind

* other than natural physical processes or known phenomena

* appearing sensitive beyond the physical world

Anything that requires sensitivity towards non-physical or supernatural natures is considered psychic work. Before we can understand psychic work, however, it must be understood.

The common ways of acquiring and processing data are represented by the five senses: sight, smell, hearing, touch and smell. These strategies are not used in psychic work. Extrasensory techniques (beyond the five senses), are used in psychic work in order to understand individuals and events. This is illustrated by the ability to read the personality of someone before they meet you. It eliminates the possibility for logically evaluating them with the five senses.

Many psychics talk about their ability to gain knowledge through extrasensory means. One example is clairvoyance. This ability allows one to see beyond the physical eye. Clairaudience (the capacity to hear without using your physical ears) and clairsentience are two examples. It might be difficult to understand but here's what you need to know:

The physical senses do not allow you to express the spiritual feelings. Emotional or spiritual senses come before the physical. It suggests that there are spiritual eyes beneath the physical eye. Spiritual ears are located behind your physical ears. Psychics may focus on these subtle operations, and then translate the data.

A psychic can pick out subtleties like the road ahead, a conversation with a friend, and the flavor of fresh strawberries. All people have the ability to communicate on an intuitive or spiritual level. A psychic, however, is someone who has been able to pick up on information that is usually ignored.

Some psychic powers start with "Clair," which in French means clear. Many psychics combine many different abilities. There are four fundamental claims.

* Clairvoyance – Clear seeing

* Clairaudience (clear hearing)

* Clairsentience (exact feeling/sensing)

* Claircognizance = clear knowing

These are the claims that are more rare:

* Clairtangency, also called psychometry, - explicit touching

* Clairgustance- Clear tasting

* Clairalience - clear smelling

What the Difference is between a Medium & a Psychic

The focus is on communication with spirits in afterlife or other dimensions, regardless if a person calls themselves psychic medium, spiritual mediums, intuitive mediums, or any other title that might be similar.

Although psychic mediums are sometimes called psychics, there is still a difference between a medium or a psychic. Although psychic mediums can be psychics, not all mediums can be. This distinction is vital because people tend to confuse the two.

Reading the past, present, or potential future of an individual or thing can help psychics tune in to their energy. For the purpose of reading information, psychics rely solely on their basic intuition and psychic ability. Mediums accomplish more.

Medium taps into the spirit energies of people to allow them to use their intuitive or psychic ability to see the person's past, current, and future. It means that the medium must have non-physical energy.

Another striking contrast is the fact that psychic readings are often focused on the future, whereas mediums concentrate on past and ongoing problems. While it can be helpful sometimes, forecasting the past can reduce people's agency. Do not forget that you have the power to control how your life unfolds.

You are free to choose your path and make your own decisions.

Sometimes psychic insight provides insight into what may happen based the current path, but it should not be used as an actual guide to help you make the best decisions.

Types and types of psychic abilities

There are many different types of psychic abilities. Some people have the ability to predict the future. Others may receive messages from beyond the grave. It is possible for some people to sense the emotions of others, or even read their thoughts.

* Precognition. This refers to the ability of foreseeing events. Some people receive clear instructions. Some may be given vague messages, such "Someone close will experience significant changes in their life."

* Intuition. This is the ability to "intuitively" know something without being explained. These intuitives have a distinct advantage in reading Tarot cards for clients because of their ability to interpret them. This is called clairsentience.

* Clairvoyance (clairvoyant): This ability allows the clairvoyant to see things that are hidden. People sometimes use divination in distant vision to find missing children and items.

* Empathy: Understanding the thoughts, feelings, or emotions of another person is known as empathy. To avoid exhaustion and weariness, Empaths should learn how to shield themselves from the energies that are being used by others.

* Mediums: These are people who receive messages from the afterlife. This can happen in many ways. Some mediums may receive messages via sound or sight while others will see visions or dream about the spirits. Some people "channel", which allows them the ability to communicate with spirits.

7 Ways to Enhance Your Psychic Ability

If you possess some psychic ability, you can practice developing them. Meditation is one of many methods that can help you develop psychic abilities.

1. Achieve Deliberate Clarity.

While this may seem complex, it's not. To have purposeful clarity you need to be alert to the world around you. Watch out for changes in light, shadows, wind and people who come and go from one area to the next. Note everything mentally. This will assist you in determining whether the messages are genuine or if they are the result of wishful thinking.

2. Pay Attention to What's Said and What's Not

People can often misunderstand what they mean when they say one thing. When your friend answers, "It's fine," when you inquire about her, she replies, "Fine." Their children are fine, but she doesn't talk about her marriage. Communication can still be achieved through omission.

3. Regular meditation is recommended.

Meditation is one of your best options to enhance your intuition. By opening up a channel for messages, your mind is able to drift into the depths and subconscious.

4. Learn to trust your gut

Are you ever unsure of what is going on? Have you ever had to turn left, when you were supposed to go right at a stoplight? You should be mindful of such things. Often those intuitive messages have a purpose.

5. Take Notes about Everything

Have you ever had dreams about a certain person, or particular circumstance? Ever get the feeling that something special is about to take place? Keep a journal to keep track of your sensory messages. These sensory messages can be revisited later to check for truth. It is possible to verify the authenticity of messages we receive from time to time.

Sometimes we receive communications that are not accurate.

6. Do it for yourself.

If you have suspicions or doubts, it is worth verifying them. Find out, for instance what music was your best friend listening to while driving to meet us for coffee. Next, inquire about her when she appears. Do you know how well you did? Consider who might be calling before picking up the phone. You can also check the CallerID to verify if your phone rings. Make sure to check your accuracy when you pick-up the phone. Engaging in simple workouts like this can improve your natural abilities.

7. Practice makes perfect

Even though it won't make you perfect, it can help you develop new skills. Learn about the different types and practice the one that speaks to YOU until you are comfortable with the integrity of the signals.

What is intuition?

Your intuition is also known as your inner voice. It is a form intuitive understanding that doesn't depend on rational thinking processes. It's a different level, an alternative source, or a voice within you, which some people have described. In varying degrees, all people have this mechanism and the ability of improving it.

Why is it important to nurture your intuition Intuition has been praised by many renowned thinkers, from Immanuel Kant to Carl Jung. Its significant impact on personal and professional life is evident. It was described as "apriori" knowledge by them, which is an explanation that is given without regard to prior knowledge. They also considered it a crucial tool for human beings.

Jung identified four mental processes that are essential to our existence: feeling, perception, thought and feeling. To reach our full potential, we must balance these internal processes. According to him, intuition can also be used to express one's creativity through literature, music, and visual art. However, intuition is not only used in these areas.

People who trust their intuitions or instincts in business, science, and entrepreneurship have made a lot of money and earned a great reputation.

Your intuition is ultimately the way you connect to your subconscious mind. It's the method through which the subconscious speaks to the conscious. It is an incredible source of insight, knowledge, and understanding. It surpasses logic's limits.

How to Improve Your Intuition

Don't think, just listen. Spend time every day in stillness. Relax your mind by using any breathing or meditation method you prefer. Do not try to comprehend everything. Listen and be open. Allow your thoughts space to wander, and then be open to the suggestions and responses that you receive. Listening to your intuition will help you connect to deeper information. It communicates with symbols, feelings, or emotions.

You can trust your instincts and intuition. Most likely, something isn't right if it doesn't feel right. One person's correct behavior could be totally wrong for another. Have you ever had that feeling in your gut where you feel compelled to do something?

You might have avoided a serious accident because you listened to your intuition. Trust your intuition. Trusting your intuition can feel scary at first. However, you will learn to trust it over time.

Stay alert and pay attention. It is important to be aware of the environment around you in order for your intuition to develop. Your subconscious mind will have more information to use when making big decisions if you are able to take in more information from your surroundings.

The more information available to you, the better the solution. Your intuition makes use of the data that your conscious mind has. Just like how experience-based insight and understanding increase the quality information offered by your intuitive abilities. Your intuition is how your subconscious mind transmits information to you.

Other forms of intuition include inspiration and fleeting ideas. Paying attention is key. More of them will come to you if your attention is more focused. You will feel the pain if your gut feeling is ignored and you are faced with unfavorable outcomes. Keep an eye out for clues and little tips to help you avoid making similar mistakes. When you're asleep, your subconscious will help you to stay awake.

Before you go to bed, think of the problems and queries you didn't solve throughout the day. Take the time to explore many options. This will boost your creativity as well as your subconscious's ability to generate new ideas while you are sleeping.

A pen and paper are essential for anyone who wakes up in the middle night with a great idea. Journaling and keeping a journal can allow you to access emotions, thoughts, ideas, and other information that you might not have otherwise. This technique can be used to reveal inner messages and insights as well as untapped information related to a particular situation or issue.

The Benefits to Developing Intuition

* Stress reduction through the facilitation of problem-solving strategies and identification.

* Unlock your creativity and imagination.

* Connects you to the subconscious, which allows you uncover hidden.

* The truth about yourself and your life.

* Connecting with your intuition is a great way to avoid unfavorable emotions and thoughts.

* This integrates left- and right-brain activities, allowing for more detailed understanding of problems.

* Increases emotional, psychological, and physical wellbeing by improving and integrating your decision making.

The process of developing intuition is similar in nature to learning a new skill. The more you practice an activity, the better you get at it. Take your time and practice slowly. You will build up your intuition muscles as you go.

To develop intuition, you need to be aware of subtle energy. This is how you can expand your awareness beyond your senses. Your intuition develops as you bring together all your senses with both your conscious mind and subconscious mind to create a complete view of the universe. In order to develop your intuition, you may want to unite your body, soul, and mind.

How to tell the difference between intuition and imagination

It would be wonderful if there was an easy way to tell the difference between intuition and imagination. There are some things you need to keep in mind when trying to discern between intuition or other things.

1. Practice and Feedback

Practitioner psychics have a greater ability to distinguish between reality and imagination because they receive more input. They are able to confirm or deny their psychic perceptions. For psychics to feel confident, they do two things: (1) practice often and (2) seek out feedback on their intuitive insights. This will help build confidence, and make it easy to differentiate between intuition and imagination.

To get feedback on intuitive insights, it doesn't matter if you provide professional readings. You only need to try them out in your daily life and notice the changes. When a voice from within prompts you into action, pay attention and notice how it sounds before you begin to observe the results. However, it is important to become detached in order to discern the outcome of using your intuition.

Many people trust their intuition and act on it. However, if they don't get validated immediately, they feel disappointed. You shouldn't approach intuition growth in that manner. Even if it is not immediately proven accurate, don't be discouraged.

Even if you're wrong you still learn because each time you use intuition and watch the results you will get closer to understanding what your specific intuitive voice or nudge is feeling. But, in order to grow psychologically, you have to accept your mistakes. Even experienced psychics can sometimes make mistakes.

2. Pay attention to the sensations that are associated with your intuition.

After some practice, it is possible to identify the distinctive energy signature of intuitive information. If you practice receiving genuine intuition, you will feel the difference in your ability to recognize the sensation of genuine intuition. Take a moment to notice how intuitive guidance makes you feel next time.

You may also receive feedback regarding how accurate your intuition through your emotions and your gut feeling about things. It is possible to tell if information is wrong or feels off to you. When I present facts you are confident in, it can make you feel positive and motivated. Inaccuracies can cause you to feel uncomfortable.

3. While intuition is passive and imagination active, it's the opposite.

Another distinction is that imagination and intuition are active processes, while imagination is passive. Your imagination is actively engaged when you create anything. When you meditate and make yourself a conduit to your thoughts, intuition can occur. You stop being active. If your thoughts are giving you inaccurate information and you want your intuition to be more in control, it's time to learn how you can control them.

You can calm your mind by stopping what you are doing. Try focusing for a couple of minutes on your breath. This can be a great way of distracting your mind to allow you to listen to your intuition. It is important to leave more room between your conscious ideas and your intuition voice.

It may not be your intuition.

* You feel discouraged, ashamed, or denigrated when the voice speaks to you.

* It sounds confusing or hazy when the speaker gives you information. Your intuitive information should be easy to integrate into your conceptual framework. If it is asking you to have faith in its correctness but doesn't make sense to you, it may be better to throw it out.

* Listen to the voice that tells you to. Intuition can be free from agendas. While intuition will offer insight from your Higher Self as well as Guides to you, it does not require you to follow the advice.

Don't be alarmed if you aren't sure. It is possible to understand intuitive messages again and again.

As you can see from the diagram, there are so many components to the human mind that it can become confusing. These topics were already discussed in introductory courses. In the next section, we will be talking about your higher selves, and how some of your guidance and communications came. In the following section we'll talk about your higher selves, and from wherece some of your counsels and communications came.

The Difference Between Psychic Abilities and Intuition

Although the words "intuition" and "psychic", are often used interchangeably they have a clear distinction. What is intuition? What does it mean to be intuitive?

Intuition can be described as a general feeling or a gut feeling. This is sometimes difficult to explain rationally. This is called "gut instinct", a "simply a feeling," and "just as a hunch". Think about your first reaction when meeting someone you don't know. Then decide whether or not to believe it.

The concept of intuition can also be described as your inner voice, higher selves, or that part of you that connects to something other than yourself. When you're still and quiet enough, the voice of intuition is audible.

Psychic information is more intuitive and in-depth. It improves your intuition and gives you more clarity and insight. One might communicate this knowledge through clairvoyance.

For example, you may be able to "see" someone's life and get information that is more intuitive than psychic.

Are you psychic, intuitive, or both?

Yes! All people have the ability to develop their psychic abilities and intuition. If you do this, you can live the life God intended and have a much easier time navigating life. This can be intimidating but it's worth it. Although this is not necessary, the majority of society today perceives the issues in question as dangerous or "out there".

If you want your intuition to work in your daily life, you need to learn how it works and trust it. It is very rare for intuitive or psychic insight to make sense instantly.

Sometimes it takes several days or weeks for the knowledge or intuition to click. It can be annoying but the wait is always worth it. Concentrate first on your intuition. Use your intuition to make intuitive guesses and hunches about your life. Then use your psychic gift to obtain more specific information.

Exercises that calm the mind and keep it quiet

The best way to suppress the constant chatter inside your brain is to practice. Being able to understand the internal process is key. You'll soon be so comfortable with the process of removing the background noise from your environment that you won't even have to do the exercise. You will be able perform it by yourself.

1. Walking on Rocks

It is possible to calm your mind with ancient indigenous practices. However, it is not for everyone. In this exercise, you will walk at a steady pace and then run slowly (once you're ready).

As you go forward on the rocks you will see that your mind will make each step a separate task. Your mind will keep going until you get tired of hearing it. After you reach a certain level of mental exhaustion, your mind won't stop telling you the right steps to take. This is when your mind quits trying to direct you in every way possible.

This point marks the end of the mental merrygo-round. It is important to take some time to be comfortable and stay here. Keep going with this routine until you are comfortable with the breaking points. As you become more comfortable, you will find the inner space where you can live comfortably without the mental merry goes-round. For maximum safety, try it on a small number of rocks on the shore instead of on high rocks.

2. Meditation

After you are able to stop the mental merry -go-round, your ability to meditate will increase. There are many meditation styles, and you must use them all to achieve the best results. It is easier to connect with the heart when you can calm your thoughts, emotions and body during meditation. As a result, your ability to reach higher frequencies will be enhanced. This is the best place to communicate with your higher self.

The messages that suddenly appear in your awareness to inspire, heal or inform you, are often coming from your higher self (or your higher intelligence) as you reach this vulnerable condition (when everything else remains still and quiet).

Additional Meditation Techniques

Meditation Journeys

However, visualization does not always have a clear goal. Meditative journeys often have one. You might be able to summon up specific images to connect with higher self, visit a island where you'll find your animal or spirit guide, and/or go to your spiritual place to review Akashic documents. You can imagine the limitless possibilities.

Visualization CDs

If visualization is hard for you, CDs will guide you. These CDs have many uses, including helping you to relax, healing physical ills, and communicating with your guides.

Meditation is about understanding that what works for one person might not work for the other. People are unique and can use many different approaches to find the one that works best for them.

4 Steps to Making Meditation Easy

1. Put Your Expectations Aside.

Allow yourself to be open-minded and unaffected by what happens when you meditate. No matter what may be happening, meditation can bring you something valuable.

Even though it does not seem to, meditation is producing positive changes in your innermost soul. These inner changes will start to manifest in your outer lives.

2. Thoughts don't have to be your enemy

How can inner peace be possible when your thoughts are at war? Thoughts, which are a natural part of meditation, can be used to release tension. Sometimes the thoughts will cease to exist. Following your method's instructions is the best way to achieve this. However, you'll soon discover that meditation can lead to profound relaxation and inner calm.

3. Relax and try to meditate.

Relaxed effort refers to the extremes of trying to get your brain working and drifting off. "Medium effort" is somewhere in between these two extremes.

4. Meditating is more fun and easier if there are less worries about what you see.

Overvaluing things can often make them more difficult to achieve.

PSYCHIC DEVELOPMENT

Our hearts are often more complicated when we live away from nature. Disregard for living things evolves quickly into disdain. As we are not in the natural environment as much, our typical perceptions are not well developed. This means that our sensory apparatus is only used in a very small proportion. This is a sign that you are able to increase your awareness and use your normal senses more effectively.

To activate sixth or psychic perception, we must first awaken the five senses, which are touch, taste. It is important to increase the use your normal senses in order to activate the inner psychic abilities. We all can put this into practice.

EXERCISE: Awakening Your Senses

1. Choose a quiet spot within nature, preferably in the shade of trees. This may be near a river, stream, or hillside. A park should be available where you are surrounded in beautiful nature even in modern cities.

2. Choose a tree with plenty of room around it, and a strong trunk. You will be able to rest your back on the trunk and still be able face the sun.

3. Now focus for a few more minutes on each sense.

Sight - Observe the sun's movement as it catches the tree leaf leaves. Note the vibrant color variations. Look closely at the colours of the flowers and bushes as well their crinkly green leaves. Feel the texture of the trunks and the hands and fingers of the branches as they are wintered. Pay attention to the clouds passing through the sky.

You can think about the way the grass is curled around your feet. Keep an eye on nearby animals, birds and insects. Keep your eyes on the sky and observe.

Hearing: Now, put all of your attention to listening. Pay close attention and pay attention to the natural sounds. Listen to the wind's rustling among the trees, bird's melodies, rustlings of small moving creatures, and insects' hum.

Touch: Pay more attention to how you feel. Feel the sun's warmth upon your face, the wind blowing on your hair, or rain's kiss on lips. You can take off your shoes, and let the soft, bouncy surface embrace your feet. Consider yourself a part the natural world.

Smell: You can smell the earthiness in the soil, the flowers' wonderful aroma, or the grass's scent. Pay attention to your sense of smell and enjoy the natural scents.

Taste: Taste (and smell) are both related senses. Your tongue will experience each flavor in the air. Due to the freshness, your taste buds might begin to react with saliva. This is a rare opportunity to connect with nature in a way that you won't have before. Spend at least five mins using your senses.

Even if you are only able to spend 30 minutes each week in peace, you will quickly notice your senses becoming more open, your creativity and intuitive abilities increasing, as well as your awareness of the spirit and things. As you do this, you will eventually be able to hear nature's sounds from a distance.

DEVELOPING PSYCHIC ALBILIITIES BENEFITS

If you have psychic talent, you can:

* Don't spend too much money or time on the trivial things.

* Avoid going down roads that take you nowhere.

• Look beyond your rationality to discover the "why", the reasons behind events, people and circumstances in your lives.

* Decide without second-guessing.

* You need to be clear about what you want and what you don't.

* You want to know how to read auras so you can discover the true natures of others.

People don't know how to listen to their intuition or to pay attention to the guidance of their hearts. Because Western culture places emphasis on science and technology, Western culture doesn't encourage or encourage listening to the ethereal, even if it is something from within. Instead, our scientific, rational culture encourages us obtain information and direction, before weighing it. This strategy is logical.

Intuition, however is often seen as unreliable and inconsistent because it doesn't compile data from many sources. Because of this, intuitive guidance is often misunderstood and not shared with others. When asked to defend or provide evidence for their opinions, most people simply say that they "just know it" or what their gut tells them. People like to hear specific facts, which are supported by proof. We often learn to abstain from speaking when our belief that we are in the knowing (without actually knowing how) is true.

By developing your intuition and psychic awareness, you can become more spirit driven than being controlled or controlled by fear or the ego. This promotes courage, growth, and confidence in all things cosmic. It is because of this that psychedelics, spirituality, and personal growth are interdependent. Your psychic abilities improve, and so does your spiritual growth. I am assuming that you already know the facts.

The Work A Psychic Does:

* Oracle and Tarot readings

* Psychic consultations, either by telephone or in person or by email

* Other divination techniques may include reading tea leaves or crystals for lithomancy.

* Leveraging your abilities to help identify any trouble spots in your client's life (human or animal).

* Telepathic communication via animals

* Psychic counseling can help people make choices about their future.

Chapter 7: Astral Projection

There are two types of Astral Projection: Out-of the-Body Experience and Astral Project.

It is sometimes called an experience out of the body. They are similar in that they both have the same meaning, but they differ in that an out of the body experience is not intentional while astral projecting is. Astral projection refers a deliberate effort to separate and send your astral or spiritual consciousness out of your physical bodies. It refers a psychic ability to allow your mind to travel through the dimensions or to other spiritual planes. Unintentional out of body experiences are more common. Your consciousness simply hovers above your body and isn't traveling through dimensions or to the spirit planes. Out of body experiences usually do not last and often occur without warning. Also, you may feel as if your body is floating and that you have altered perceptions of the environment. You will also feel like you're looking down at your self from above.

Many cultures recognize astral projecting as an ancient practice. You can use it to learn more about the spiritual planes, and to strengthen your spiritual connections. While astral projection and transfiguration may sound complicated and difficult, it is not impossible if one puts their mind to it and practices regularly. Once you've mastered it, it'll be a rewarding spiritual skill.

Astral projection is, as we know, the ability to voluntarily project one's astral body. It involves falling into a dreamlike condition while being awake and aware of your surroundings. Also, you can use the power of your brain to travel to other realms in both time and space. It's a similar experience to being in a nightmare, but you are fully awake and aware.

Astral projection is based around the fact that all of us have astral bodies. They are sometimes called our energetics, etherics, subtles, or spiritual bodies. Additionally, there is an astral realm (or spiritual realm) that extends far beyond the physical realms that we are currently living in. If you are doing energetic healing, then you may already be familiarized with your energetic andtral body. A person performing an astral projected connects to their astral physique to allow them to transcend their physical body. The astral body allows them to mentally navigate through time and space.

Although astral travelling is a great method to explore new realms or new places, it isn't an easy skill to master. It takes practice and a lot of patience to get it right. Learning astral projection can be a rewarding experience. It will allow you to release yourself from the physical confines that are imposed on your body.

How to Perform Astral Projection

It is not possible to teach astral travel or any other psychic skill. There are no instructions that can be used to teach astral projection. Because everyone has a different experience with it, there are some guidelines that we should all follow. You should first master astral projecting before you can start your astral travels. These practices will allow you to get in touch more etheric areas of your consciousness.

If this is your first time astral projection, it may be a good idea for you to try some meditations. If you don't have a regular meditation practice you can add a few minutes to your daily life. You might also consider using essential oils or crystals to meditate if it is difficult to calm your mind.

Once you're comfortable meditating regularly and have developed a habit of doing so, you can then start practicing self-hypnosis for deeper trance states. Self-hypnosis is a way to access the astral planes. This allows us to make connections with others. Self-hypnosis has many similarities to meditation. You go deeper into the astral body to perform self-hypnosis. Once you have focused on a goal or intention, such as performing astral projections, you begin to see the world through your eyes.

Once you are able get into a deep and peaceful meditative Trance, you can move on to connecting with your Astral Body. While you are still meditating, visualize your traveling body. This is a more transparent representation of you, and it will lift up from your body. Once you have that mastered, it's time to start turning your head and seeing your astral self. This might not happen immediately but you can keep practicing and remain patient. If this doesn't happen naturally, you can visualize your astral self and align yourself with it consciously. If it takes you many meditation sessions to feel truly connected, do not be discouraged. Keep in mind that every person is different.

Once you feel safe in your astral body and comfortable, you can start to communicate with the astral level or the unlimited mental space beyond what is contained within the physical world. The astral plane can be connected and aligned through meditation, visualizations, controlled breathing, and letting go our consciousness, while still being fully aware of what is occurring. A deep meditation that induces a trance state, where you think of a specific person or situation, can allow us to travel through space, time, and dimensions beyond our bodies. It allows us to see the world differently and unite with others. Once you reach this point, it is possible to begin to move through space and connect with other energies, ideas, dimensions, and spaces in time. This can be done by combining your intuition, astral body awareness and meditative meditation.

If you achieve the state while practicing, it's time to go on your journey. Once you have successfully connected to your astral self, you need to be conscious of the intention to go to a place. It is best to enter your astral plane with an intention or goal in place. You will not be wandering aimlessly. One intention might be to contact a spirit guides, visit a place from the past, or find spiritual answers that are not available in the material world. Perform astral projection with caution and cleanse your energy before each session. This will ensure that you don't pick up any strange vibes or messages.

After getting used to astral travelling and feeling confident in your ability of accessing your astral bodies and moving around on the astral plan, you will be more able access this state. If you want to achieve your goal, then practice is key. If you have been performing astral voyages for a while, you can just do a simple mediation to allow your consciousness to travel to the other astral planes instantly. Even though you might not always reach the destination you desire or may not be able access the astral realms with ease, the more you practice the more your ability to astral project.

Lucid dreaming and dream interpretation

What is Lucid Dreaming and How Does It Work?

People often dream without realizing that they are dreaming. They don't realize they are dreaming. During a dream everything feels real, and we wake up to find out that it isn't. However, psychics are capable of being able enter a dream while fully conscious that they are dreaming. A lucid nightmare is a dream where the dreamer is conscious that they are dreaming. These are dreams in which your consciousness is awake and you are conscious that you are dreaming, but your body still sleeps. Your brain is aware that your dreams and flashing images are not real. Even though you feel the dream vividly, it is not true. Sometimes, your dream may turn out exactly as you imagine. This can allow you to control the dreams you have when you're having nightmares.

Lucid dreams can occur most often in Rapid Eye Movement or the REM phase of sleep. This phase is characterized with fast breathing, rapid eye movements and increased brain activity. The REM period is usually reached around 90 minutes following the time we fall asleep. This lasts initially for 10 minutes. As you sleep longer, each Rem phase becomes longer and more prolonged. Finally, it can last for as long as an hour.

Lucid dreaming is a great way to reduce anxiety. The feeling of power and control you get from lucid dreams may stay with your even after you wake up. This can make it easier to feel empowered. If you're aware that you're dreaming, you can decide what the dream's story will be and how it will end. For people having nightmares, this might be a way to get rid of them. Lucid dreaming can also improve motor skills. According to some studies, it may be possible to improve small things like being able tap your fingers more quickly by practicing it while we dream. The same brain regions are activated when our brains are thinking about the movements of our fingers while we are awake or just dreaming.

Also, lucid dreams can improve our problem-solving skills. Lucid dreams are able to help you solve problems which involve the creative part of your brain. This is a way to have a better relationship with others, rather than solving problems that require logic or math thinking. This means that lucid visioning can help you increase creativity. If you're lucid dreaming, it may even be easier to find a better idea about something.

Lucid dreaming doesn't always bring good things. In fact, it could make your sleep less quality. Lucid nightmares can wake you up and make you unable to go to sleep again. Also, lucid dreams can make it harder to sleep at night if you keep your eyes on them. Lucid dreaming can also lead to confusion, hallucinations, even delirium for people who have mental health issues. For them, it may blur the lines of reality and fantasy. This could make it difficult to tell if something is actually happening or not. It can also lead to a loss of sanity.

Methods to Increase Your Odds of Having A Lucid Nightmare

1. Reality Testing

Reality testing is the act of pausing for a few seconds at different times of day to test whether you are awake, asleep, or in a dream. It is possible to try doing something that is impossible in the real-world, such as pushing your finger into your hand or trying inhale/exhale while covering both your nose/mouth. Try to do something you don't normally do in a dreams. For example, try reading a page from a book while covering your nose and mouth.

2. Write A Dream Journal

According to some reports, dream journaling can make it easier for people to have lucid dreams. A dream journal by itself may not be sufficient to aid you in lucid dreaming, but you can use it to combine other methods.

3. Instantly Wake up and Return to Sleep

You may be able get back into REM if you wake up after you've slept for just five hours. It will increase your chance of experiencing lucid sleep because lucid thoughts are usually experienced in REM.

4. Use Mnemonic Induction For A Lucid Dream

Mnemonic stimulation is the act of telling your mind what your next nightmare would be after you wake up from a five-hour sleep. This activates your prospective memory. It is the act of recalling what you did in the past to increase your chances of having lucid dreams.

5. Take Lucid Dream Inducing Drogues

Many drugs, such food supplements and medicinal plant can have an effect on our sleep quality and how we feel in dreams. However, this can lead to lucid visioning. It is not recommended because we aren't sure if they work well or if they are safe.

6. You can try using devices that induce lucid dreams

Use masks or headbands that create a particular pattern of sounds and lights to induce lucid dreaming. An alternative to recording yourself is to use your phone to record yourself telling yourself that you are going back to lucid dreams. This will help to remind you that you are dreaming.

Other Types of Dreams

1. Daydream

All types of dreams are happening while we're asleep. However, daydreams can happen in the middle of your day while you're awake. Although you may be aware of daydreams, it might feel as though you aren't fully awake and aware of what's happening around your. A daydreamer may appear to be lost in thought or completely lost. Daydreaming is usually about other people. Daydreaming about people who you are close to can help you have a more positive outlook and may even be associated to better health. However, daydreaming over people that you do not know can lead you to feeling lonely.

If you aren't careful, excessive daydreaming can lead to a decrease in productivity and other negative consequences in your daily life. Your daydreaming may have a positive effect on your life in certain situations. It can increase productivity and help you focus better. However, if you do it excessively you could lose your attention and forget important information. If you are working at your job and need to focus on your task, daydreaming could cause you to lose your concentration and slow down your work. Daydreaming while operating heavy machinery can cause serious health problems for you and your coworkers.

If you have too many negative daydream thoughts, daydreaming can lead to mental health problems. While most people daydream about the things they desire and dream about, some daydreamers might think about what it would be like to do something to harm themselves or others. Reports have shown that suicidal individuals may be driving down the highway, daydreaming of crashing their car into something or someone else. These kind of daydreaming fantasies may be quite complex with lots of details. It almost feels like they are planning an actual project, not just a daydream. If it is something that could harm you or other people, daydreaming can be very harmful for your mental well being.

Daydreaming can, however be used to your benefit if it is done in moderation and properly. Setting aside time each morning to daydream is one way to do this. Daydreaming can be done in many ways. You can choose a time that is convenient for you and set it. This mental exercise can help you relieve stress from a long day at work. This can also be used to calm down after an argument with someone close, such as a friend or a family member. Daydreaming can be a great way to deal with traumatic events in your life.

Daydreaming allows you let go of all your worries and lets you forget everything for a little while. This practice can be a great way to maintain your sanity in difficult situations. Even if the situation is temporary, you can escape it and come back to that situation with a positive attitude.

Daydreaming can not only help with stress but also allow you to stay calm and relaxed. Daydreaming lets your mind take a break from all your worries for the time you set aside. You'll often feel rejuvenated and refreshed after your daydreaming session. This happens because you allow your mind time to rest and stop worrying so much. Most of the times, this small break is all you need to be able go back to the task and complete it. Working on the same task for too long can cause boredom and make it difficult to concentrate on. Daydreaming can allow you to take a break from stress or pressure. In the end, you'll feel refreshed and ready when you return to the task.

Another option is to use daydreaming in order to manage conflict. This is what's commonly called organized daydreaming. It involves imagining different scenarios that could be used to solve a current conflict or prepare for future conflicts. By properly using daydreaming, you can review various situations with your mind and be prepared for all possible outcomes. Imagine you have a daydream about the possible outcomes and how you would react if someone tried to rob, as you return from work. It is possible to organize daydreaming so you can think of different scenarios so you are prepared in case it does happen. Make sure you only dream about things that are possible. You don't want to fantasize about having super powers and taking out the person trying to rob.

Daydreaming is a great way to maintain relationships. If you can daydream about spending time with your friend or romantic partner while you are apart, it can give you the feeling that you are still together and they are right there. You can daydream, imagining the times you had together in the past. Or you can daydream about what your future plans are if you do meet up again. Imagine that your partner has moved to another part of the country for work. You will be unable to live with them for several months. However, you could daydream about what it would be like to be there. Daydreaming will never be the same thing as meeting those special people in life. However, it can help deal with loneliness.

You can also daydream to help boost your work productivity. When you take a moment to daydream about a problem you are facing at work, or any other situation, you might find a number of possible solutions. It can improve your mood, and overall make you feel more positive. A positive mood and feeling good will increase your productivity. If you don't feel well, then you may become exhausted and not be able to focus or do any work. Daydreaming helps us to be more motivated to complete our task or job and move on to the next one. Daydreaming increases motivation, productivity, and can even help us reach our goals. Visualization is a good tool to help you reach your goals. It is a well-known method for athletes and high-achieving people such as CEOs or CEOs of large corporations. Daydreaming, visualization, and daydreaming can be very effective for all people.

Daydreaming can help to concentrate and set higher goals for yourself. Your ultimate goal in life will help you to focus and achieve it. It is possible to reach your goal quicker if you use daydreaming in moderation. Daydreaming is often viewed as a way to escape and do nothing. But you can make it work for you if you learn how to properly do it. Daydreaming will increase your creativity, problem solving skills, and allow you to concentrate on a particular task. It lets your mind wander to places and thoughts that are not possible if you don't have time to do it. If you are using daydreaming in your favor and are using it effectively and efficiently, it can be an extremely powerful technique that can help you reach the ultimate goal of your life.

2. Nightmare

Nightmares may be disturbing dreams or nightmares that make it difficult to wake up from a nightmare. It is common for people to experience nightmares every now and again. You may have one or more of these possible causes:

* Read something frightening or watch a horror movie.

* Eating too many meals right before you go bed. This leaves your stomach not enough time to digest your food.

* Not getting enough sleep, feeling tired and uncomfortable

* Side effects caused by the medication you're currently taking

* Feeling sick or experiencing a high temperature

* Other sleeping disorders such sleep apnea where your breathing stops and starts again, narcolepsy which makes it more difficult to remain awake for long periods of times, and nightmare disorder

which causes you nightmares that are extremely frequent.

People who are stressed or have mental disorders such as anxiety can experience terrifying nightmares. People with PTSD and post-traumatic Stress Disorder are more susceptible to having nightmares that recur if treatment is delayed. The following are some of the most common nightmare themes.

* Run away from people or things that are trying to chase/hunt you down

* While you're watching, someone is hurting you.

* The death or dying of someone you know or the death of yourself

If you're having nightmares frequently, some lifestyle changes may help. If you find yourself having nightmares often, you might try to get more exercise.

Try to encourage your child to tell you the stories of their nightmares. Encourage them to openly talk about their dreams whenever they dream about anything. They should be able to tell you that these nightmares will not harm them in any way. Also, it is not something they can expect to experience in the future. Your child should have a regular sleeping routine. They should go to bed and wake up at the appropriate times every night. To help your child relax, you can teach them deep breathing exercises and make sure they do not experience nightmares.

3. Night Terror

If someone has a night terror, they can wake up scared and stressed. Most often, it's the latter. Night terror victims will not be able to recall the dreams they had. Night terrors can make it very difficult to wake up. You may experience a coma, shaking, sweating, rapid heart beat, severe dizziness, and disorientation. It is possible to have both a nightmare and night terror. The main difference is that nightmares are more vividly recalled dreams, and nightmares are less easily forgotten.

Because children have less non-REM sleep, night terrors are more common. But nightmares can strike anyone, regardless of their age.

4. Recurring dream

Recurring nightmares are dreams you keep having. These are often dreams related to being chased, dreams concerning a confrontation, or dreams about falling off a high place. There are two options: a neutral recurring dream or a nightmare. It could be related to a mental condition or substance abuse. For a dream to be considered a regular one, it doesn't need to be identical each time. A dream may depict you driving a car over a long bridge. However, the bridge suddenly collapses during your drive. It is possible to have another similar dream. Even though you drive a different car on different bridges, the bridge still collapses while you are driving. This would be considered a recurring dream. You might find that a recurring nightmare can begin as young as a child. As a result, it may change slightly over time due to the changes you've experienced and how your world views have changed.

The belief is that recurring dreams could reflect your most important life issues, such as your unmet or frustrated needs, past experiences, or any other problems you may have. A dream you might have about not being in a position to complete your research paper on the deadline or missing an important exam could be an example. Even though you may have had this dream while you were still a student it could be a result of stress that you suffered. It can also happen later in your lives, even after graduation. This dream can be related to your dreams of success and your anxieties about failing at something. You may experience this type of dream whenever you are confronted with similar situations. This could include a job interview. A bad dream that makes you upset the first time you experience it can make you feel worse. Repeating the same nightmares multiple times could cause you to feel even worse. You cannot always control the dream contents, but it is possible take indirect actions and try to solve the problems which are causing the bad dreams. No matter your situation, a professional counselor can provide guidance to help you manage stress and take care of you. In therapy, you can identify and explore the causes and effects of any unhappiness or emotions you are feeling. It will also teach you how to deal with stress and anxiety. Although it is unlikely that you will be able to completely eliminate the stress you are experiencing, it is possible to change how you respond to it. This will help you have a better outlook on your life and make you more optimistic about your future.

5. False Awakening

False awakening describes a type dream where someone may believe that they have woken from a dream, but in reality they are still in a dream. It's similar to having a dream within a dreams because you wake up from a fantasy only to discover that you are still dreaming. If you ever have woken from a dream and it remains part of your dreams, then this is a false awakening dream. Some people have multiple false awakenings happening at once. False awakens can be related with sleep disorders such as insomnia and sleep apnea. You may also experience false awakenings due to the anticipation of waking or knowing that you will need to wake up earlier for a specific reason. Stress and anxiety can impact your sleeping quality and cause nightmares. If you're worried about something happening soon after you wake up in the morning, you may dream of waking up and facing the problem. These stressful events might include a difficult exam and a job interview. False awakening is not considered a cause of medical concern, although it might feel strange. False awakening is not an indication of any health condition. But, it's worth checking into any problems that might be affecting your sleep. False awakenings could occur in conjunction with other symptoms that may have a more serious cause. Talk to your doctor if you're experiencing other symptoms such as difficulties falling asleep or staying awake, fatigue after a long day, excessive sleepiness or nightmares.

Improved sleep quality can help to reduce false alarms. By turning off your phone at least one hour before your bedtime, you can improve the quality of your sleeping and decrease the frequency of false awakenings. The disturbing dreams you have can be caused by anxiety or depression. These conditions may also affect your sleep quality. A professional therapist is recommended for any mental health symptoms that are not improving after a week.

6. Vivid Dream

A vivid dream is almost always related to waking up during the Rapid Eye Movement (REM), phase of your night. This is where your dreams are the most vivid and easily remembered. Although vivid dreams can technically be considered all dreams experienced in REM, vivid dreams feel more real than regular dreams. It's also easier to recall vivid dreams than regular dreams because of the intense feelings that were associated with them. Vivid dreams can result from sleep disorders such narcolepsy, insomnia, and other sleep problems. A vivid dream can also be caused by changes in your sleeping habits, such as when you travel abroad and go to sleep at a different time than usual.

Vivid dreams are usually not something to worry about. However, sometimes they can be detrimental to a specific part of your daily life. Negative vivid visions can be disturbing especially if they continue for a longer time. The most common side effect to vivid dreams is daytime insomnia. This can cause you not to be able focus on what you are doing and your concentration may drop. It can also lead to memory problems that could affect your productivity, whether you are at school or at work. Vivid dreams could even impact your ability for daily tasks, like driving to work or getting to the bathroom. Even the simplest task can be extremely dangerous if it isn't your primary focus. Vivid dreams are also very draining. They can bring on intense emotions which can cause depression and anxiety disorders. This can be extremely concerning, especially if you have vivid dreams that last for a lengthy time. This could be because you're afraid that another vivid vivid dream will occur.

7. Healing Dream

A healing dream can be described as a dream that restores harmony and balance in your mind and body. It helps you feel connected, fulfilled, and connected to your purpose and life. It happens when your dreams are about happy things that make you happy, and you feel good even after you wake up. Your spirit guide can help you to achieve this. If you feel that you need some support, your spirit guides can help you find a soothing image or a childhood memory that will make your dreams more pleasant. If you feel like you require a heal dream, you may be able to ask them for help. If you are able to communicate more with your spirit guide, and have a strong connection, you can ask them for help in your day. Asking them to help you with a dream of healing is one example. It is possible for your spirit guide to grant your request, as long as you do not cause harm to them or other people. After you have resolved a major conflict, it is possible to experience healing dreams. This will give you the feeling that a lot of weight has been lifted from your shoulders. This will allow for you to relax more easily and to get better sleep. It can also increase your chances to have a healing dream.

8. Prophetic Dream

Prophetic dreams are dreams that psychics are able predict the outcome of future events. If you have a prophetic dreams, you may dream about a specific scenario. If you have experienced a certain event in your dream, you might experience a sense of déjà vu. Dreams can be an important tool for receiving wisdom from God and can even help us predict our future. Some believe that a dream that is prophetic is our subconscious trying out to predict a particular event. This then causes us to have dreams about the situation to help prepare. The reality is that prophetic dreams are sent by the spiritual world. They help us to manage certain situations and guide us on how to react. This type dream could be a message from the spirit world to warn you of a danger approaching you.

Although most prophetic dreams show us the future in the near future, it can also tell us what is happening now that we are not aware. It is a message of the universe, which is meant to assist us in dealing with a situation. Imagine that you have a dream about a friend that uses illegal drugs in order to get help with a particular problem. This dream may be happening right now or in the distant future. It is sent to your friend to help him deal with his problem. Prophetic visions are sent to us to save ourselves and help us avoid making the wrong decisions in our lives.

Interpretations of Dreams

Although experts have studied dreams for many years, they are still very misunderstood. Many people don't know how to interpret the meanings behind the images and scenes we see in our dreams. While we are asleep, the mind is still very active creating scenes, stories, images and scenes that can be vivid, blurry, and instantary. It may seem to give us a glimpse into the future, be absolutely terrifying, totally routine, or bring joy and peace to help you relax and stay calm.

Symbols, signs and phrases are the main language in a dream. Dreams may not always be literal. Every detail of your dreams is linked to a different part of your daily life. Every symbol in a nightmare can bring you a different feeling.

However, sometimes we are left confused by these symbols and wonder what their meanings might be. Knowing how to interpret dreams, or those of others, is a powerful tool. You will be able help people to better understand themselves and their emotions. As you analyze someone's dream, it is possible to learn more about their deepest feelings and desires.

If you interpret your dream on your own, it is the best method. Because you know what happened and how it felt when you were dreaming, and can understand yourself better than anyone else. It is crucial to consider every detail in your dream. Each symbol represents a feeling. Be attentive to the characters and places that appear in your dream. You can interpret even the most insignificant details of your dreams.

List of Common Dreams with Their Meaning

1. Have a great time falling

It is common to imagine yourself falling from a high place. Most people have had the experience. One common misconception is that falling from a high place in a dream will cause you to fall and then you will eventually die. But this is simply not true. What does it really mean to have a dream about falling? According to many dream interpretations, dreams of falling from high places can be a sign your life isn't going as well as you would like. You might need to rethink how you live your life or look at a different direction. You might feel too overwhelmed, out of control, or insecure. The falling in your dream is a sign you need more time to enjoy your life, relax and let go of certain things.

2. Dream about being Chased

If you feel that someone or something is following you in your dreams, this could be extremely scary. The idea of being chased is a dream that you're facing a difficult issue in your life. However, you don't know how. It could be that you are trying to avoid something. It is crucial to understand the details and motivations behind your dream. If you feel like you are being chased down by a monster, it could be a sign that you are suffering from an addiction or indiscretion. If an animal is following you, it could be a sign that you are hiding anger, passion or any other feelings that you wish to suppress. It is possible that the one that is following is a shadowy or unidentified figure. This could indicate a negative childhood experience, or past trauma. If the one chasing your is someone of the opposite sexuality, it may indicate that you are fearful of falling in amour or haunted by a past relationship. If the person who is after you is someone you have known personally, it is possible to draw more insight from your associations than the reality of the person that is following you. Be aware that you can use other people in your dream to replace people or a part of yourself. Your dream about someone following you may be an indication that you need to confront your fears and pursue a goal you have put off.

3. Do you dream about dying?

Another common dream topic is death. This is something you should be concerned about. Sometimes, you may have a dream about the death if someone is close to or close to you. Sometimes, your dream may include you dying. As with death, change is also scary. It is not always clear what is next. That is why death in dreams can signify that you feel something is coming to an abrupt end in your life.

A dream about the passing of someone you love could indicate a fear of change. This is a sign that your child is growing up. When parents worry about this, they may start to worry about their children's future. Even though it is not the same as before, their kid is still there. Dreams about people close to you may reflect a mourning phase for the inevitable passing time.

Pay attention to how you feel about the death in your dreams. Your dream may indicate that you are ready and able to let go of something that is not right for you. However, if you feel scared or panicked in your death vision, this could indicate that you aren't quite ready to let go of something.

4. Your Teeth Will Fall Out!

The dream of your teeth falling out dreams can have many meanings. Many people can have it many times. Your physical appearance, or your sexual attractiveness, could be the reason you dream about teeth falling out. It could also indicate that your ability to communicate with other people is at risk or that you may have embarrassed someone you have met in the past. As a result of anxiety, dreams about your teeth slipping could be an indication that your fears are becoming reality. This could be your anxiety about not being able to reach your full potential, not being competent enough, not having the strength or the power to take on the world. This dream could be caused by a major life event, such as the loss of a job.

The appearance of our teeth is a representation of how powerful, confident and in control we feel. When your teeth fall out in a dream, you lose your personal power, your confidence, and the ability you feel to be in control, assertive, decisive, and in control. It is a common dream you have when you are going through transitions or times of change in your own life.

5. It's possible to dream of being naked in public

Are you familiar with those embarrassing dreams that you have had where you're in public areas like school or at work, but you don't wear anything? When you realize that it is not a real dream and you are not naked in public, you feel great relief. These dreams are not uncommon and common. You might dream about your naked self in public. It could signify that you are feeling vulnerable and worried about being exposed. It is possible that you feel untrue to yourself, or that your shortcomings and faults might be exposed. It could be time to learn how to gain confidence, to be comfortable with sharing yourself with other people, and not worry about what others might think. If you've ever had a vision about being naked in public that made you feel confident and free, this could indicate that you would like to be accepted and admired for who you are and the things you do in your life. You might desire to be more visible than you are.

6. Flying is something that you can dream about

Many of our dreams involve flying. This type dream can be extremely exciting and entertaining. Some people may even feel freed by this dream. But, for many others, it can also be frightening, especially for someone afraid of heights. You can have dreams about flying that represent independence or freedom. However, you might also dream about flying as a way to escape daily realities.

Sometimes we dream of flying by ourselves, which is a sign of independence. However flying also brings us positive feelings of pleasure. It can also show aspects of our sexuality. When you fantasize about flying it means that you are freed from something that is hard or frustrating. A problem that has been weighing down your life for a while is now gone.

If you feel scared when you fly in your dreams or see something in front of you, this could mean you feel blocked or prevented from doing the thing you really want. It is similar to the feeling you get when something seems close to taking off, but it is not yet there. It is like you're close to something but can't seem to get it. This could be a new relationship or a dream job. Look at the details of your dreams. It could be a relationship or a job that you really want.

7. Dream About Infidelity

It can be very distressing to fantasize about your romantic partners cheating on or with you. In some cases, others may even wonder if it is possible for their partner to cheat on them. It could be that your partner is cheating on yourself, or it could just be a dream. Sometimes, this type of dream can be a sign of your partner cheating. But it doesn't necessarily mean that your partner will cheat on me in the future. You might have dreams about your partner cheating. This is simply a sign of not receiving enough of what is important to you or what you desire from the relationship. This can be a sign to have a talk about your relationship with your partner and to give them a chance to express any concerns you may have about your relationship. As long as it doesn't make you angry at your partner, or make them feel guilty about what they did in real-life and in your dreams. The act of dreaming about your partner cheating means that you are telling your partner you need to change something. You and your partner can spend more quality time together.

Dreaming that your partner is cheating on you could also mean that you have other feelings. These feelings may be related to your desire to escape or try something new. You could be having a difficult relationship with yourself. There may be a desire to leave your current job and live in a remote area. This type of dream could also refer to simple ideas like starting a project on your own or learning something new.

8. The Dream of Seeing an Empty Room

A dream that shows you an empty room could mean you have a hidden talent. The more time you spend exploring any talents you might have that aren't known, the greater chance you have of finding more opportunities.

However, if there is fear or discomfort in the room, it may be a sign that something else is happening. If you are having a dream about going into an unoccupied room and feel scared or scared, then it might be that you have discovered something new about yourself. It could also be something you were not paying enough attention to in the past, but is now troubling you. It could be related any area of your life, including your job or the relationship you have with a friend. Open the door even though you are afraid so that you can face your fears.

9. Think About Going To An Important Exam

You might have a dream that you will take an exam. This could be an indication of a fear of failing or making mistakes. This dream is usually linked to the current work you are doing. It is because we were students in school when we first got our job. It's common to dream of taking an important exam if you are facing a challenge at work. If you feel well-prepared for the exam, then you will feel confident about the challenge that lies ahead of you. You will feel confident that your efforts will be rewarded.

Exams are stressful for us because it forces us to confront our faults and weaknesses. If you fantasize about failing an examination, being late, or not being prepared, it can also mean you are unprepared for the work challenges you are facing. However, it is possible to use your fear of failure and make mistakes to benefit. You can use this fear to drive you to work even harder to complete the tasks you need. Fear of being not prepared can serve as inspiration to help us get ready to do the right things with confidence.

10. Have a great time dreaming about seeing a snake

Dreams of seeing a snake often represent a toxic person, situation, or person. However depending on the details of your dream, this snake might sometimes signify something completely different. If you felt fearful after seeing the snake, it's likely that you are feeling anxious about a person or situation in you life. If you are bitten or bitten by a snake in your dreams, this could indicate that you need medical treatment. If the snake bit you in an area of your body, it could be a sign that you need to have physical healing. It could be that the snake is climbing up to your body and signaling that you have energy issues in that area. If the snake keeps appearing in your dreams over and over, then it is likely that you have been overwhelmed by a toxic individual or situation in your current life. You may be seeing the same snake over and over in your dreams. You see the same snake more often in dreams. This means that it is more prevalent in your current situation or person. Even the type of snake that you dream about has an important meaning. You may see a rattlesnake when you are dreaming. This could be a warning signal or red flag that something has already happened to someone or a situation. Garter snakes can be a warning sign that a situation or threat has passed. The garter Snake is not a poisonous species of snake. While it might represent someone you are cautious about at first, you will find that this person is not likely to cause you any trouble. Depending upon the location, the meaning of where you saw the serpent in your dream can vary. A snake that appears in your bedroom can indicate that something or someone is very close to you. Because our bedroom holds a lot of importance, it is possible that the snake could be related to that person or thing. A snake found at work could be a sign of something that is troubling you or making you feel uncomfortable.